THE ANCHORHOLD

A Divine Comedy

THE
ANCHORHOLD

A Divine Comedy

By
ENID DINNIS

Who showeth it thee? Love.
JULIAN OF NORWICH.

ST. AIDAN PRESS, LLC
Morning View, Kentucky

The Anchorhold: A Divine Comedy.

First published in 1922 by P. J. Kenedy & Sons, New York.

Typesetting, layout and cover design copyright 2014 St. Aidan Press, LLC.[*]

Cover art by Katherine Rabjohns and Andrea England.

ISBN-13: 978-0-9719230-3-4
ISBN-10: 0-9719230-3-5

For more information, contact:
www.staidanpress.com
staidanpress@gmail.com

[*] Text reset and proofread in 2024. We have made no intentional change from the 1922 text except to correct spelling and punctuation mistakes.

CONTENTS

To

Dame Julian of Norwich

THE ANCHORHOLD

Chapter I

Most of the Game

FIDDLEMEE, the jongleur, sat on his little wooden stool behind the high table, midway between the festal board and the buttery-hatch through which the busy servers accelerated the business of feeding my lord the baron's guests. He doubled a long blue leg over a red knee and, stooping, whispered something into the ear of Flipkin, his dog, who, like Orpheus, the lute, accompanied his master wherever he went.

Fiddlemee's was a point of vantage, albeit a humble one, for observing all that went on at the high table, which had not yet occasion to requisition the services of the jongleur; the guests were so far entertaining each other, and incidentally entertaining Fiddlemee, an inversion of the accepted order of things which tickled his fancy not a little. He had strolled round the high table with his wooden stool in his hand, his bright, impudent eyes scanning the different pairs of guests—there were perhaps thirty or forty seated at the banquet with which each day of the great tournament was brought to a close—and he had finally taken up his position near the spot where the old, very old baron with the long white beard and a long white reputation, was conversing with his partner, the Lady Editha de Beauville, to the envy of the sublimely beautiful young knight opposite. The shaggy old veteran had the reputation of being a bore of the first degree, but he had succeeded in engaging the entire attention of the Lady Editha, the wittiest woman of all that select assembly. She was evidently interested in what he was saying—her singularly expressive countenance reflected the mind of its owner with extraordinary vividness. The young man opposite had forgotten his own partner and was listening to what the two, or rather the one, was saying. It was a suggestive little drama to an onlooker with eyes like Fiddlemee. He stooped down and whispered to his partner. He lifted the end of the ear that had been allowed to flop by one of Flipkin's motley progenitors and remarked in a discreet undertone: "His ancient lordship, the elderly baron, is playing a brave melody on my lady's lute. 'Tis a finely strung instrument, and methinks Sir Galahad is mighty envious of the player. 'It was a gallant knight that loved a lady fair,'" he chanted softly: "but Sir Galahad will have to play a braver tune than my lord the old baron's to win the lady's hand. How now, Flipkin, doth not the onlooker see most of the game?"

The dog cocked his head. He was a curious blend. Square-chested and consequential in front, thanks to a bull ancestor, with negligible hinder quarters. Wholly and entirely consequential in his own estimation, Flipkin's imperturbable effrontery made him very kinsman of the jongleur.

The latter continued his observations as he watched the faces displayed in full profile as the lady and her partner conversed. He surveyed the arresting countenance, the features of which showed a curious independence of the canons of beauty. Like the Lady Editha's mind they went their own way, and withal produced a result with which orthodoxy could pick no quarrel, inasmuch as the end was achieved. No one ever looked upon the Lady Editha de Beauville without arriving at the joy which it is beauty's business to create.

The old baron's discourse was evidently on some interesting topic. Fiddlemee addressed the listener, *sotto voce*. "Have a care, lady fair," quoth he, "so tender a countenance should be spared the wear and tear of telling thy soul. Methinks thy fair cheek will grow sunburnt from within. So bright a light shines there, dear lady, that soothly thy fair cheek must already be befreckled on the inside!"

Young Sir Aleric's eyes were likewise fixed upon the listener, whose listening possessed so vital and vivid a property. "Sh-ush!" Fiddlemee mouthed at the baron. "Not so loud, not so loud! I want to hear the lady listen. Now, I wager thee, Flipkin," he went on, lifting the dog's ear, "that the baron tells the tale of King Richard offering himself to the insurgents as their leader after they had slain poor Wat, who had slain the archbishop. The lady, so sayeth my good grandmother Rumour, hath great ideas about the people's well-being—she hath freed all her villeins since she became lady of the manor. My lord the baron will be telling her that he was with the King, that many years ago, for he is mighty proud of it, is the baron, albeit that King Richard (God rest his soul) did but strike an attitude, or so they say who have not truck with our good Mother Charity."

Flipkin was frankly bored with the confidence. He flicked his ear, which tickled, and kept his pink-rimmed eye—the one without a patch round it—fixed upon the figure of my lord baron, the host of the occasion, who from time to time cast a sweetmeat in the direction of his mad jongleur. These Fiddlemee caught deftly and divided into two equal parts with scrupulous exactitude, one for Flipkin and one for himself. The punctiliousness of the division sometimes tried Flipkin's patience. His master was not pernickety as a rule.

There came a lull in the buzz of conversation. Others beside Sir Aleric had ceased from their own chatter and were listening to what the old baron was saying to the Lady Editha, or rather to what she was saying to him, for she had got a word in at last, it seemed.

Her blue eyes were shining like stars, and there was a delicate pink flush mantling her cheek. The Lady Editha's voice was low-pitched and vibrant, one heard it the better for its very gentleness. It contained a very decisive quality. The de Beauvilles were a clan who knew their own minds, and who enjoyed that privilege exclusively, for the world never quite knew to reckon what a de Beauville might not do next.

"But," she was saying, "the prince was not as good as his word. It was indeed a grand thing that he essayed, but he stopped short at the idea. He was a coward if he were not in sooth a hypocrite." At the latter word my lady's blue eyes flashed. The two words, coward and hypocrite, were as flint and steel that produced fire.

"Nay, nay, dear lady," the old baron responded, "that is the hard judgment of youth. The prince was in sooth confronted with the idea and he fell in love with it. He would verily have pursued it but circumstances were against him, and he lacked the strength to overcome them."

The lady meditated. "Had he accomplished it," she said, "had he indeed led forth that army of the weak and misled to freedom it would have been a finer victory than Agincourt." She paused, and her eyes flashed starlight upon the listening assembly, or so it seemed to Sir Aleric whose own were wide open at the amazing dictum.

"Have a care, have a care, fair lady," Fiddlemee entreated. "So much shining will fade the colour of thine eyes. Prithee, remember that thou art a lady and not a lanthorn!"

The surrounding guests sat and absorbed this latest ebullition of the de Beauville peculiarity exhibited in the heiress. The very calmness of her voice, of its low vibrant tones, held them spellbound. Each forgot his or her allotted companion and listened.

Sir Aleric felt the hot blood mount into his brow. His rival in the tourney lists, the only one left between him and victory, was seated near their host, next to His Reverence the King's chaplain. He and Sir Gervase would settle the question of supremacy tomorrow in the final encounter, and afterwards the victor would offer his guerdon to the Queen of Beauty. There, in very sooth, she sat, opposite to him, a vision of delectation, of beauty too elusive for analysis. No painter could catch that something that flickered over the faulty features and gave them a charm that was verily beauty itself. Beyond he could see the thin, shrewd face of Fiddlemee, the mad jongleur, with his sharp brown eyes, regarding the scene; his dog Flipkin's head was thrust out between his ridiculous knees. The old baron's eye had likewise kindled. "Yea, in sooth," he said, "there are finer victories to be won than Agincourt, but who are there that would win them? The prince saw his vision, so do many others, but no man hath the power to make it good."

"But the vision remains," the lady said, "others may make it good. Thy prince was a poltroon. He was given his vision and his lance remained at rest." Her lips tightened. There was a dreadful sternness now in her shining eyes. It sat with a strange incongruity on the curiously delicate face.

"Did'st thou ever see a flower frown?" Fiddlemee enquired of Flipkin. "Tell me, what dost thou think became of the bluebell that was inhabited by a martial spirit? Lady, lady," he went on, shaking his head at the speaker, "thou wilt grow old. Never was thy fair face made for such wear and tear of thought. Heaven send thee no visions, for soothly thou wouldst ride out full tilt, and maybe disarrange thy fair locks."

The silence was tense. The high table had been bewitched. The heiress of the de Beauvilles sat there, a figure almost as transparent as the diaphanous head-gear in whose folds it was framed. Her eyes had become like unto the sapphires in the fillet which held the shimmering drapery in place. The room held no such rare picture amongst all its gaily dressed assembly. The banality of the prevailing type of beauty—a type that befittingly paraded itself in costumes that had been specially designed for the occasion, was thrown into pitiless relief by the woman who by her scornful independence of the fashion had achieved that most to be envied of

5

charms—uncommonness. A charming woman, reigning in splendid isolation. The eyes as well as the ears of many would-be queens of beauty were turned in her direction. Youthful, witty, unwed, and the richest woman in the county, Lady Editha was not unused to attracting attention. She proceeded to carry her point calmly. "King Richard's vision lay in front of everyone possessing feudal power. The poor who suffered wrong still looked for a leader, if it were not King Richard it would be Wat, the sacrilegious murderer of God's priest."

My lord, the president of the feast, being a man of tact and discretion, became alarmed at the turn the conversation was taking. It savoured of Lollardry, and His Reverence the Chaplain Royal was his guest. He called to Fiddlemee. "Come, now, thou rascal, and sing us a song. A cheery song of doughty deeds to suit our mood."

"Something braver than Agincourt," an ironical voice suggested. It was the voice of Sir Gervase, the world-champion at the joust, Sir Aleric's remaining rival.

Fiddlemee sprang up and mounted into his place. He glanced at the Lady Editha. They were acquainted, for she had taken much notice of Flipkin. He rested Orpheus on one knee—the red one—and began:—

> "Rag and Tag and Bobtail, shouting of its wrong—
> What a pretty mob tale for a minstrel's song!
> Rag and Tag and Bobtail, Rag—Tag—Bobtail led,
> He must be a true king who would be their head.
>
> Rag was erst a swineherd, Tag was erst a clown,
> That would be a fine herd to escort a crown!
> Bobtail was a jongleur out to earn a meal—
> Each a pretty bungler with the soldier's steel.

Most of the Game

England's gallant bowmen schooled to act as one—
Picked to face the foeman, every mother's son,
Fashioned of the breed that follows where it's led,
Fiddlemee could lead that standing on his head!

He must be a monarch, he must be a man,
Who would Rag, Tag, Bobtail weld into a clan.
With a heart to draw them into battle line—
With a soul to awe them with a heavenly sign.

Rag forgetting Rag's wrong—Tag forgetting Tag,
Though his wee world wags wrong following a flag.
Bobtail out for something bigger than his bray—
Agincourt's a glum thing 'gainst that doughty Day!"

The singer paused and crossed his blue leg over the red one. "Now,
a song for the ladies," he said, and broke into the following:—

"Maiden, maiden, sigh a wee,
Flitting sighs nor long enduring
Speedful are to lover-luring.
If so be,
Maiden, maiden, sigh a wee.

Maiden, maiden, weep a wee,
Tears nor yet too strongly salted
Move the heart where words defaulted
If so be,
Maiden, maiden, weep a wee.

Lady, lady, think no thought!
Brows bewrinkled lie in waiting
On the art of meditating
Rightly taught,
Beauty even would be shrinking
From the wear and tear of winking.
Lady fair beware of thinking—
Lady, lady, think no thought!"

The baron turned to his august neighbour, the royal chaplain from Windsor, who was to preach at High Mass on Sunday at the termination of the tournament. "'Tis a quaint fellow that," he observed. "He maketh up his songs on the spur of the moment, both rhymes and tunes. A curious trick he hath, and methinks not a common one." The good baron had suffered many qualms during the past recital and felt that Fiddlemee's song might need an apology to the prosperous cleric, for was not the spirit of Lollardry in the air? "The fellow is as mad as a march hare," he went on. "That maketh him passing droll. I have no need to bemuse him with wine to get merriment out of him; in sooth he refuses to take it in case, he saith, being already mad it should make him rational. A queer, quaint fellow. He practises his religion like a monk. I have no fear for his loyalty to Holy Church."

The chaplain seemed interested. "Where didst thou pick him up?" he asked.

"On the roadside," the other replied. "He told me he was the King's jongleur—a most audacious lie, as I afterwards found out, but the poor fellow evidently regards it as a pleasantry. 'Tis a joke without a point as I can see, but he sticks to it. I put him in the stocks when I first found it to be false, but after all it is part of the poor fellow's craziness that makes him amusing, so I hold him not to blame that he persisteth in it."

The prelate smiled. He was inwardly tickled at the thought of the rather pompous baron being in mighty good conceit of himself at having secured an ex-royal domestic for his retinue.

He chuckled at the story of the jongleur's craziness with great affability.

"Suppose," he said, "thou introduce the King's jongleur to the King's chaplain."

The baron called to Fiddlemee. The latter approached and dropped humbly on to one knee. Flipkin set his head jauntily on one side and invited the cleric to toss him something from his plate.

"So I hear that thou wert the King's jongleur once upon a time," the Chaplain Royal said. "I have no recollection of meeting thee at Court."

Fiddlemee was ready with his answer. "The King's jongleur," quoth he, "is ever at the King's elbow. Thy Reverence may not have climbed so high."

"In sooth thou hast impudence enough for thy trade," the other remarked, good humouredly.

"Impudence is part of my duties," Fiddlemee answered gravely, "just as sanctity is part of Thy Reverence's. Did I behave respectfully to Thy Reverence, my master the baron would have me whipped. Unlike Thy Reverence I am permitted to be sanctified only when I am at play."

His Reverence grinned widely. He had a humorous twist of his own, and was a sportsman to boot for all his holy calling. He enjoyed this passage of wits with the mad jongleur.

"Then in thy playtime," he retorted, "I presume that thou makest sermons? Come now, Sir Jongleur, thou hast a handy wit. Make me a sermon to preach when I lack a handy one of my own making—in thy recreation time."

Fiddlemee bowed. "Thou hast great wisdom, reverend father," he said, "in entrusting the task to a jongleur and not to a holy clerk, for thou wilt thus be safe, in very sooth, from detection, for didst thou preach a discourse of my making, and did the world get abuzz with its fine theology, and poor Fiddlemee lay claim to its authorship, folks would but say, 'Beshrew me, but the mad jongleur is madder than ever!'"

The cleric had been handling one of the sugarplums in the dish before him. Flipkin, watching the suggestive action, grew restive and gave a short, sharp bark to recall His Reverence to the point, as it appeared from Flipkin's mental angle. "Thy dog and thou art well matched," he observed, laughing, as he flung the sugarplum in Flipkin's direction.

Fiddlemee dropped on to his knee. "Thy blessing, holy father," he said. "The feast is over, they are calling on thee to say the grace. It is my play hour arrived. I pray thee bless the King's jongleur."

The other hesitated a moment. Then he raised his hand and gave the jongleur his blessing. Flipkin sat with his lip curled up crunching his sweetmeat between his white teeth. From the high table there came the clatter and clang of tongues and jostling cups. "Play well," His Reverence said, for he was a holy man none less than a sportsman.

Chapter II

Finer Than Agincourt

SIR ALERIC'S PAGE had vested him from spur to pennant in his knightly garb, and a formidable warrior he looked. True, the point of his lance had been crowned for the friendly rivalry of the lists so that no further injury than that of unhorsing might be inflicted upon his rival. And verily Sir Gervase, champion of all the rings in Europe, had got to be unhorsed or else how could Sir Aleric, lord of ten thousand acres that he was, proclaim the Lady Editha Queen of Beauty? How gorgeously she had merited that title last night as she sat there talking to the old baron. In sooth Sir Aleric had received his high commission—to proclaim the very queenhood of the matchless lady who had gazed out with wonder-ridden eyes from the festive board at a vision of something "braver than Agincourt"—of a feat finer than the great victory still fresh in the minds of Englishmen. There were many fair ladies present at the tourney. She had only then flashed out, as it were, in the fulness of her mysterious beauty, a woman by herself, with the traditional dignity of the imperious de Beauvilles investing the slight, fragile figure with all that pertains to a commanding presence. And yet had not the mad jongleur described hers to someone as "the kind of face that one would discover within the petals of a violet did one walk in a garden that was enchanted." This "lady alone" had a færie touch about her. She seemed to dwell aloof from the personalities surrounding her so that, wherever she might be, her dwelling-place was

Wonderland, across whose borders one gazed but might not step.

Sir Aleric's esquires found him very distrait, but small wonder. It was a momentous occasion, this the final test of his prowess. As he stood waiting for his horse in the court leading to the tiltyard there approached Fiddlemee the jongleur and his egregious dog. The former ran his eye critically over the magnificent figure of the knight-at-arms. He wore his visor up and the fine, statuesque face was visible. He might easily have stood as a model for Sir Galahad, the knight of the Grail.

"Remember, Sir Knight," the jongleur admonished him, "thy feat of arms has to be a braver thing than Agincourt or the Queen of Beauty will hold her champion as stark nought. The lady's soul is a lute upon which thou must play a braver tune than e'en did my lord baron if thou wilt win her ear."

"That was a brave song thou gav'st us last night," Sir Aleric said. "Didst thou in sooth make it up on the moment, Sir Fool?"

"Which song might it have been that pleased thy Gallantness?" Fiddlemee enquired. "The blue song or the red song?"

Sir Aleric drew his brows together interrogatively. His wit was less subtle than that of the King's chaplain.

"That is," Fiddlemee explained, "the song I sang with the lute on my red knee, or that I sang with the lute on my blue knee? 'Tis to suit myself to my master's mood that I sport one red leg and one blue."

Sir Aleric scanned the thin, dark face with its ascetic cast of feature. "Dost thou verily make up thy songs to suit the occasion?" he repeated.

"'Tis thy humble servant's one gift," Fiddlemee replied. "So doth Heaven compensate him for othersome foolishness. A light talent for a light-headed rogue, but a talent, none the less. So I can sing you my songs as you will them—on my blue leg, or on my red leg. 'Tis the same thing to me, for 'tis but one song I sing whether on the left leg, or the right. For, see thou, I can give thee jam and powder, or powder and jam—'tis the same fare. Cheese-and-bread or bread-and-cheese—'tis the same thing, yea or nay—'tis the same thing."

Sir Aleric laughed. "Ask a lover," quoth he, "whether yea and nay mean the same thing when he awaits his lady's answer. Come now, Sir Fool, I will give thee a silver talent if thou wilt prove to me that yea or nay be the same thing to him in such a case."

Fiddlemee regarded the speaker critically. "Thou art a good Christian knight?" he said, interrogatively. "Thou wilt stand by thy bargain?"

"So I will, good Christian knight that I am," Sir Aleric replied. "So now, Fiddlemee, answer me my riddle and earn thy talent."

"And that I will, right readily," Fiddlemee answered. "Doth the lady answer, yes—'tis the will of God. Doth the lady answer, no—'tis likewise the will of God, Sir Christian. So doth both yes and no mean one and the same thing. Two songs, that is, the one that I sing merrily on my blue knee, the other sedately on my red knee, but for all that it is the same song—a song of the will of God."

His bright eyes twinkled at the knight as he held out his hand for the talent.

"Thou rogue!" Sir Aleric cried. "Thou hast wit enough, though it may be misplaced in thy head. Take thy talent, thou hast slain me with my own rapier."

"Yes," the jongleur replied, "and it hath been done right cleverly, for thou hast been pierced by the hilt and not the blade." He pointed to the cross hilt of the other's sword. "But I may not take thy talent," he went on, "for to take money in return for spiritual chattels were the sin of simony." He rejected the proffered coin and vanished into the stable, above which was his lodging, followed by his dog.

"A queer fellow," Sir Aleric thought, "I wonder if he hath always been a jongleur?"

The tilt-yard was surrounded by the gaily-draped gallery accommodating the spectators. As he rode into the lists, Sir Aleric glanced up at the place where the Lady Editha was seated. She was dressed in blue velvet, and her head was veiled in gossamer draperies—blue over green, reminiscent of the atmosphere of a dell peopled by bluebells. There was that in the queenliness of the Lady Editha which did not entirely exclude Queen Mab.

"Is she indeed there, or am I dreaming her?" Sir Aleric asked himself as he gazed up through the sight-holes of his visor at the tapestry-bedecked balcony. "Methinks," he added to himself, "that it would be a fairer lot to dream of her in a hermitage than to wed any other."

Then he pulled himself together for the great effort that was to crown her Queen of Beauty. Sir Gervase, the champion who roved about Europe, from tourney to tourney, throwing down his gauntlet to those most skilled at the joust, waited on the other side of the tilt. His reputation was at stake, for Sir Aleric was but newly sprung into fame in the tilt-yard, though a warrior with no mean record for his years. The contest began. The lances of the rivals met. The swift, sudden manœuvres of the mounted opponents met with full appreciation in the galleries. The women understood the points of the joust as thoroughly as the men. It was an intent audience.

Suddenly there was a *contretemps*. Something had gone momentarily wrong with the harness of Sir Gervase. His rival's opportunity was there—the unhorsing of Sir Gervase, and victory. The latter's attention had been diverted for the fraction of a second, it might be, but sufficiently to afford the opportunity that no jouster could have failed to turn to an abiding advantage. But the opportunity passed. The countenance of Sir Aleric was hidden within the visor above which fluttered the cognisance which betrayed his identity, but that of the Lady Editha, who was watching the mimic fray with breathless intentness, was visible. Her amazingly swift perception had noted the faint suggestion of a checked movement, and she knew that Sir Aleric had deliberately foregone his opportunity, true knight that he was. Her eyes became as twin sapphires.

The little episode was not lost upon at least one of the spectators, the ever-observant jongleur. He noted the turn of the young knight's head when the round was over and he knew that his eye was seeking the Lady Editha. She knew it too, for she was smiling at him with such sweetness as the observer had never seen there before. He addressed his comment to Orpheus, his lute, failing the presence of Flipkin.

"Beshrew me," quoth he, "but the true knight hath played a fine tune upon the lute up yonder. He hath gained a mighty victory. I tell thee, Orpheus, he hath done something finer than Agincourt."

There was a general feeling of regret that the new champion, Sir Aleric, failed in the end to come out victor from the joust. Sir Gervase succeeded in unhorsing his rival in the encounter that followed the one above recorded. Perhaps it may have been that Sir Aleric had been bemused with a draught from his lady's eyes, and Sir Gervase had not scorned to take advantage of the untoward happening, but, however it was, Sir Gervase rode out victorious to receive the trophy from the lady of his choice.

Sir Aleric stood by when the Lady Editha bestowed the trophy, for she it was whom Sir Gervase had named Queen of Beauty. He felt in his heart no envy of his rival. Had he not gained something a thousand times more thrilling than victory at the joust? He stood within range of the lady's eyes with a strange light upon his own countenance, and as she bestowed the trophy the lady raised her eyes from the figure of the kneeling champion and looked upon the one who was second in the lists, so that her words might well have been addressed to him. They exchanged a smile—the Queen of Beauty and the fair knight who bore a likeness to Sir Galahad of old—and the latter found himself in heaven, as he stood there witnessing the triumph of his rival.

Fiddlemee the jongleur watched it all as was his wont.

"All goeth well with thee, Sir Knight, save an one comes along and plays a yet nobler strain upon His Majesty's lute. 'Tis to the champion at the joust that the fair lady will give herself. God help thee, Sir Knight, if a nobler comes along."

The banquet that night was a more gorgeous affair than ever. In sooth the reader may feel grateful to the chronicler for not entering at length into details of the feast provided, a thing which were but done to exhibit his due acquaintance with the manners and customs of the period.

Fiddlemee fingered his lute impatiently. He had a song to sing, and there was a twinkle in his eye when he looked at the complacent countenance of Sir Gervase, the champion. It would have gone badly with Sir Gervase in his own estimation had he been beaten by this fair-haired youth that looked as though he should have worn a halo to match his locks.

When the jongleur's moment came he sat himself on his perch at the end of the table and started his ditty with a few brisk chords of introduction,

> "Pride and Pity went a-jousting,
> For to gain a gilded laurel.
> All the ladies in the city
> Came to look at Pride and Pity
> Settling of a family quarrel.
> Gallants gay and ladies witty,
> List, my story holds a moral.
>
> Pity's lance can eke, I trow, sting—
> Pity's stroke sent Pride a-reeling.
> Oh, but it was sorry jousting!—
> Pity felt his native feeling.
> Pride's sick wound takes long in healing,
> Pity's wounds no gangrene show.
> Oh, but it was sorry jousting!

Pity, ere the great stroke dealing,
Checked his hand and stayed the blow.
Oh, but it was sorry jousting
When Sir Pride escaped his ousting,
Sat up straight, and roundward wheeling
Struck, and laid Sir Pity low.

Pride rode from the lists a victor,
Pity rode behind his foe.
All the ladies, kind and pretty,
Vowed it was a great, great pity,
And I wis well it was so—
'Twas in sooth a great, great Pity
That the knightling Pride laid low."

He ran his eye over the company. The Queen of Beauty was
applauding vigorously, comprehension dancing in her eye. Sir Aleric was watching her with a countenance full joyful. Had Heaven
ever assorted a goodlier pair of lovers the king's chaplain had asked
himself, as he sat watching the significant byplay to the drama of
the Queen of Beauty. He had enjoyed the jousting with the others.
He sat at the festive board that evening on the right hand of the
presiding lady. He was to preach at the High Mass on the morrow, and it was beseeming that he retired in good time to prepare
his discourse, for he too had a professional reputation to keep up.
He was said to be one of the finest orators in the Church. He had
made many attempts to slip away from the revel but the fun was fast
and furious and time passed swiftly. Sir Aleric, still occupying the
heaven which was his now whenever within the range of the Lady
Editha's smile, was seated opposite to him. The young knight surveyed the royal chaplain and assigned him a place in his day-dream.
He wondered if it would be His Reverence who would tie the knot
which would make Sir Aleric and the Lady Editha man and wife.

At last the holy man contrived to withdraw himself from
the alluring surroundings. In the upper gallery leading to his

bed-chamber he was accosted by the jongleur—the mad fellow who had engaged him in the verbal sparring match the night before.

"How now," the cleric said, rather shortly. "It is late, and I have no time to give thee, my good fellow," for he saw that the other was wishing to say something.

"Pardon, holy father," the jongleur said, "but I have here to give thee that which I did promise Thy Reverence." He thrust a sheet of paper into the other's hand.

The cleric had no conception of what he was alluding to, but rather than prolong the interview he accepted it with all courtesy. Fiddlemee vanished promptly, and the other sought his chamber.

The hour was late and the chaplain's head was dazed with the noise and clatter of the feasting. He sat himself down and there and then fell adozing. When he pulled himself together it was dawn. His lamp still burned. Fiddlemee's mysterious paper was still in his hand. He opened it in curiosity. It contained, in small but neat and clerkly writing, the synopsis of a discourse—text, heads, reflections, all complete. At first he was bewildered. Then he remembered how he had twitted the rogue by telling him to write a sermon in his play-hour. The impudent fellow had taken him at his word! Well, if only he could be as prompt in fashioning a discourse for the morrow which had all but arrived all would be well.

Chapter III

The Field and the Treasure

OURNAMENT SUNDAY was a high festival, albeit not one marked in the calendar. The parish church, where High Mass was celebrated with special magnificence, was thronged with worshippers. The white walls of the sanctuary were hung with tapestry, and seats in the tribune accommodated the guests from the castle. The enclosure, that is to say, a railed-off portion of the nave where seats were provided for persons of quality, was also filled with visitors who had foregathered for the tournament. Behind them the village folk, and those who had tramped in from the surrounding country, knelt in the clear space assigned to them. Through a tiny window which pierced the chancel wall obliquely the holy anker who inhabited a cell built up against the church did his share in assisting at Mass. At the end of the nave, close to the west door, knelt Fiddlemee, the jongleur. The Lady Editha occupied a seat in the tribune, and Sir Aleric blessed the kindly fate which had placed him where he could obtain glimpses of her for the edifying of his soul. Devotion had already lighted up the lamp in her eyes as she knelt there, intent on her orisons, a very devout lady, as the wife of every true knight should be, thought Sir Aleric, precipitating matters.

When sermon-time arrived the appearance of the King's chaplain in the pulpit was greeted with breathless attention. His majestic figure and clear-cut features were matched by a voice of unusual richness and beauty, which he controlled with the genius that makes of oratory a fine art, apart from the thing spoken. With the words of his text the audience became rapt in attention.

"The Kingdom of Heaven is like unto a treasure hidden in a field."

The words were not of necessity familiar to gentry seated in the tribune, though many of them possessed their Bibles in the Latin tongue, with which they were acquainted. To some of the simple folk in the nave they might have been new if they had not happened to have been made the subject of a miracle play, like other of the parables. The juvenile section of the congregation pricked an eager ear. Treasure hidden in a field! Of a surety the Divine Teacher knew what appealed to human nature.

The preacher embarked upon the story of the man who had private knowledge that a certain treasure lay buried in a certain field, but in which part of the field he could not tell. He must needs buy the whole field and then turn it over, rood by rood. The price of the whole field would absorb every penny that he possessed, but the treasure was assured did the field once become his. So he gladly paid the price, in spite of the protests and advice of his friends. For them the field possessed no points. Poor soil, stubble, no pasture—what could he want with it? And why was he so serenely satisfied with his bargain? They saw him running here and there, seeking to realise on the utmost of his possessions so that he might obtain the required price; and at last the price was forthcoming and the field was his. The preacher told the story dramatically, and when he had worked his hearers up to a high pitch he broke off into the spiritual meaning of the parable. "What is this treasure? Ask the saints. Eternal life? Yea, and a joy in this life surpassing the joy understood by the ordinary man. Where is this field? What is the price of the barren acres purchased by him who buys them with all that he hath?

"The Kingdom of Heaven is like unto a treasure hidden in a field." The glorious voice, with its perfect intonation reiterated the cry, and the undefined yearning that it roused in the heart reverberated through the audience.

"What then are these possessions that we set such value by? Our wealth?—the price of a field wherein lies buried a treasure. That is its intrinsic value. What is the value of our high estate, our power over others? A purchasing value—the price of a treasure buried in a field. The cost of those barren acres beneath the stubble of which the treasure lies buried."

He asked the question for the third time. "What is our liberty—our right to choose our own way—make our own life; what is the intrinsic value of this right to choose as it appears in the sight of the holy angels? The value of a treasure buried in a field. By possessing choice we possess the power to renounce choice—the wherewithal to buy obedience, abjection—to purchase renouncement. 'The Kingdom of Heaven is like unto a treasure hidden in a field.'"

The preacher's eye travelled over the brilliant assembly. The knights in their glittering paraphernalia of arms; the ladies in their gorgeous robes. He was no friar, yet he was preaching renouncement—the hard saying of the cloister. It came the more startlingly from the domestic prelate of the King's Court.

Sir Aleric listened. He experienced the thrill produced by the ringing words. And with the thrill he experienced a sudden pinch at the heart. He glanced across at the Lady Editha with a feeling of sudden apprehension, and fear shot a dart that tingled through his being. The Lady Editha's eyes, like everyone else's, were fixed on the preacher, or rather on the place from whence the voice came, for they were not looking on the man but on something else—the vision of a treasure buried in a field. Wide open eyes, big with wonder, eager, like a child's, and strangely child-like in their wistfulness. Yet it was no child, but the heiress of the House of de Beauville. Queen Mab had a crown and sceptre to barter, the wherewithal to buy treasure valued above crowns. There was a light in the "seeing" eyes that was as that generated by flint and steel. The parted lips set themselves in a firm line. The lady's eyes turned towards Sir Aleric, but they were looking beyond him—beyond Master Anker's little window at his back.

"In the name of the Father and of the Son and of the Holy Ghost," the preacher said, and his hearers stood up to participate in the *Credo*. Sir Aleric, good knight that he was, laid his hand upon his sword. What a Faith it was to defend! What a vision to die for, that which she had gazed on out beyond the anker's window.

The Mass proceeded with all the pomp and ceremony of full liturgical rites. A man of the world making a hasty inventory of his assets might have found all represented here. Wealth, beauty, rank, honour. Each of the senses, sight, hearing, scent—tasted a sample of the delights accorded to it, sanctified and sanctioned, in the brilliant robes of the clergy, the sound of the music, and the sweet odour of the incense. "The Kingdom of Heaven is like unto a treasure hidden in a field." All these and how much besides of his loves, his joys, of his very self, must a man sell in order to obtain the price of a treasure buried in a field of stones and stubble?

They had reached the *Sanctus*. The great folk in the tribune bent low in their draped benches. At the far end of the nave Fiddle-mee knelt, his hood thrown back showing his crown, shaven even more completely than those of the clerics. He scarce dared to bend himself with the others at the showing of the Host lest the bells attached to his garments should mingle their profane tinkling with the sacring bell.

Outside the church Flipkin huddled himself against the closed door, shivering with self-pity and whining softly now and again. He scraped the sturdy, nail-studded oak ever and anon with his paw. Flipkin never understood this, the sole occasion for separation from his master.

Mass over, the villagers gathered outside the church door to watch the quality depart. The horses of the latter were in waiting beyond the lych-gate of the "God's Acre." They emerged, gay and glittering in their silks and velvets, and made their way along the path lined with open-mouthed spectators who might well marvel at the amazing toilets affected by the ladies who honoured the event of the week by an affectation of the military in their garments. Their tunics were girdled, and small, jewelled daggers attached to them. Some even affected the divided skirt in their daytime attire.

In striking contrast to these came the Lady Editha. Curious eyes were turned to obtain a near view of the "Queen of Beauty" who had been so named by the victor of the joust. She approached with Sir Aleric in attendance, and a noble pair they made. He with his fine figure and broad shoulders, and she not a whit less majestic, albeit that she barely reached up to his shoulder. She had a gentle word and a smile for the children who pressed round her, regarding her as a sort of princess from a fairy tale in her pale green robe with its golden girdle, a gracious, womanly figure, thrown into relief by the tawdry brilliancy of those with which it was associated. There was a rough, weed-grown path branching off from the one they were traversing. It became a mere beaten track amongst the graves and threaded its way round to the north side of the churchyard. The lady questioned her escort concerning it.

"Oh, that leadeth to the anchorhold," Sir Aleric explained. "Master Anker has his habitation amongst the tombs round on the other side of the church."

She gave a little shudder, and he changed the subject. "It was a fine discourse," he said, "and finely delivered."

The lady inclined her head, but she did not elect to discuss the sermon with Sir Aleric. He had a feeling of having shrunken to the size of one of the children on the pathway on whom she had smiled so kindly. And now she was smiling kindly upon him, and that rather accentuated the impression. There was just the feeling that a cold shadow had flitted down the anker's path and passed between them. It had been but a shadow but it had made a gap, and the gap remained.

His Reverence the Chaplain Royal was reciting his office in the pleasance near the castle keep when he received an intimation that the Lady Editha would conceive it a very great courtesy if he would call upon her in her bower some time that afternoon. The good father was more than ready to comply. Like everybody else he was absorbedly interested in the Queen Mab lady, with her arresting charm and unusualness, who was the heiress and spoiled child of the famous de Beauvilles, who were all interesting enough to be termed "mad." No one could ever say what a de Beauville would do next, or cause others to do by sheer weight of personality. Consequently he lost no time in presenting himself at the lady's apartments.

His Reverence found the Lady Editha seated in solitude. She was demurely gowned in soft but shimmering dove grey that shot out pinky rays when the wearer moved her lissome form. The Lady Editha was in pursuit of ghostly counsel. The King's chaplain was fortunately at hand, very fortunately, because the de Beauvilles were accustomed by a transmitted habit of mind to seek what they required on the moment. The King's chaplain, moreover, would seem to be the right person to consult, having experience with ladies of high degree.

The Lady Editha came to the point at once, it being her habit to obtain what she was in search of by the shortest and most direct means. Had she lived five hundred years later the Lady Editha de Beauville would have fully appreciated the qualities of an engine unknown to those rude days, the tank to wit.

Her eyes were as bright and as eager as a child's but her manner was perfectly—exquisitely—composed. She welcomed her visitor with all due graciousness and deference, and having invited him to be seated embarked upon her business. It concerned the sermon that His Reverence had preached that morning. His Reverence looked as though he wished it might have had some other purport, but evidently he was there to discuss business arising from his discourse, so there was nothing to be done but to abide by it.

"I want thee to tell me," the lady said, "how anyone wishing to—to follow that same ghostly counsel would be moved to act? Supposing it were someone with very great possessions." She fixed her twin sapphires upon him questioningly, and the delicate pink of her cheek deepened, just a shade.

The priest felt about for an answer. It was quite impersonal. He was in no wise acting as a spiritual director. He proceeded to make this plain. "I suppose," he said, "anyone in that position—feeling the call—would enter religion as a monk or a mendicant friar, most probably the latter in these days." With considerable subtlety he had applied the male sex to the hypothetical personage.

"And in the case of a woman?" the Lady Editha asked.

"In the case of a woman," His Reverence opined. "I should imagine that she would probably found a religious house and gather together a number of pious women to live there under her rule. Where a woman possesses a gift of commanding others it is no mean vocation to lead them up to her own spiritual level. 'Tis a talent with which one must needs traffic, that of leading others."

The Lady Editha sat silent. She twisted a magnificent ring round and round on her finger. She was turning his words over in her mind, and they were evidently not ill-pleasing. The royal chaplain had not intended that they should be. The advice he was proffering was quite impersonal, in no sense spiritual direction and, after all, a court chaplain is a courtier. He continued in the same strain: "Where such a one possesseth wealth and land whereon to establish a convent and becometh abbess, it also giveth great opportunity of aiding the ill-condition of the poor. A lady abbess with a large and enlightened mind may, in sooth, be no small power for the working of good to the common people in the country-side wherein she ruleth."

The picture had evidently impressed itself on the Lady Editha's sensitized mind. The betterment of the common herd was the great dream of her life. To unite it with this other thing was surely an inspiration not to be passed by. She sat listening with absorbed attention to the many further things that the theologian had to say. He was a man of learning and a proficient exponent of ascetical thesis, and he warmed to his subject as he discoursed to his inspiring listener. In sooth she seemed to draw out of him things which he scarcely knew to be in himself, and withal, at the end, she thanked him very gently and sweetly for his ghostly help.

The royal chaplain took his leave on the whole well pleased with himself. He had directed her new-born ardour into quite the most suitable channel. Who would have dreamt that the morning's discourse would have had so amazing a result. That there was nothing ephemeral about the lady's decision he felt convinced. The straight, almost hard line of her mouth as she weighed the pros and cons betrayed a determination that would stick at nothing. It was hard on the young knight, her suitor. He had apparently made so sure of his conquest. He started in the midst of his cogitations for he had suddenly come upon the jongleur and his dog. He turned and walked swiftly in the other direction. He had no desire to encounter Fiddlemee at that moment.

It was not Fiddlemee's lot, however, to be avoided by all the quality. It might have been a couple of hours later that there appeared, walking across the courtyard, the figure of the Lady Editha de Beauville. She was devoutly veiled and carried a large vellum-bound book of orisons. She was on her way to the chapel to pray. The jongleur surveyed the bent head and the dove-coloured robe and prayer-book.

"His Reverence the King's chaplain hath been making sweet music upon my lady's heart-strings," he whispered to his confidant, "but methinks he doth not know the bravest tune, and he can only play the tune which he knoweth. Now, Flipkin, I wonder what tune he hath been playing upon my lady's soul?" At that moment the lady caught sight of the jongleur and called him up to her. He knelt and kissed her hand, for there was such wondrous sweetness in her face that, in sooth, any would have done the same. She made some kind enquiries as to his dog, for all dumb and helpless things appealed to her. Flipkin answered the question in person. He placed two soiled paws on the front of the delicate robe and wagged his long tail with great cordiality.

"Down, thou varlet!" Fiddlemee cried, "keep thy foul feet off the lady's gown."

"Nay, nay, scold him not," the lady said, casting nevertheless, an apprehensive glance in the direction indicated. "Flipkin and I are great good friends."

But Fiddlemee's attention had suddenly become diverted by something that lay on the ground. It was a lump of mouldy bread, thrown out from the bake house. He stooped quickly and possessed himself of it. The lady noted the action, and the eagerness which had made him so far forget his manners as to turn his attention whilst she was yet conversing.

She was concerned. "Surely, good fellow," she cried, "thou art not going to eat that! They do not starve thee, do they, Fiddlemee?"

"Grammacy, no," the other replied, "the jongleur lives on the fat that drips from his master's table. This is for Master Anker, up in the cell by the church. He dependeth upon alms for his daily bread, and during joust week few remember his existence so that the poor fellow is like to go short and starve. This very morning he was in a parlous way from fasting, but this will do him well. His holy palate hath preference for that which is dry, and a trifle mouldy."

He had roused the lady's interest. "Tell me more about this Master Anker," she demanded. "Who is he?"

Fiddlemee shook his head. "None knoweth," he answered. "They do say that he was a man of wealth and of high lineage who sold all that he had and bought a field." His bright brown eyes looked shrewdly into hers. "He has lived in yonder cell for well-nigh thirty years, and none hath unlocked the door. He tells of ghostly things to those who go thither enquiring, for some do say that having bought the whole field, and having dug for thirty years, he hath found therein a treasure."

The lady regarded him meditatively. "Thou wert evidently in church this morning," she remarked.

"Yea," Fiddlemee said, "near to the door. Flipkin was right outside, but holy Mother Church hath decided that the jongleur hath an immortal soul."

She was deep in thought. "I would fain visit this Master Anker," she said. "He surely could tell one many things—you say he doth expound ghostly mysteries to those who visit him." Her tone was eager and imperative.

"Yea," Fiddlemee replied, "but the way to his cell is rough. The pious pilgrims go thither, but as an act of penance." He glanced at the robe that Flipkin had so nearly disqualified, and at the lady's dainty footwear.

The spoiled child of the house of de Beauville ruminated on the situation; then she decided. "I will go now," she said. "Tell them to saddle my horse."

"But the holy man may be engaged in his orisons," Fiddlemee objected. "Thy highness may have her ride for nothing. He doth not always speak with one."

"He will speak with me," the Lady Editha de Beauville answered, with the quiet confidence of one whose experience of the world of men does not include holy anchors. The strange blue light darted from her eyes.

Fiddlemee argued no further. "I will tell them to saddle thy horse," he said, accepting the office of serving-man as part of his duties, "but the path to the cell will have to be traversed by my lady's feet. Let her see that she is fitly shod."

He bowed himself double and disappeared.

Chapter IV

Master Anker Maketh Music

The Lady Editha's serving-man waited with her horse at the gate of the churchyard. The lady herself, her dark riding-habit held up above her well-booted ankles, picked her way along the beaten track between the doleful mounds that led to the north side of the church. She turned the corner and saw the anchorage in the distance built against the chancel. It was a bleak, forbidding situation. Unbaptized babies and those who laid violent hands on themselves were buried there under the heaving turf. A grim yew tree cast a shadow over the path which led along the gray wall to the anchorage.

The Lady Editha had pursued her way swiftly and determinedly. Now she halted and scrutinized the gray excrescence with something like fear. There was indeed a door to the building but it was overgrown with moss and clinging ivy. The thought of a living being within was calculated to strike a chill upon the heart. The Lady Editha drew her breath quickly as she approached the little window. There was a stone slab beneath it, and a rough seat to accommodate the visitor. She stood hesitating what to do next. The desolation of the place had gripped her impressionable soul. She would fain have turned and fled, but turning and fleeing was not a quality of her race. She approached the window and knelt upon the stone slab and tapped softly on the window-ledge.

Presently there was a shuffling sound within, and there became visible through the window a shaggy white head. Master

Anker used no curtain to his window. The head receded quickly and a thin, very gentle, rather quavering voice asked: "What wouldst thou, my child?"

The direct simplicity of the question appealed to the applicant. Her reply was equally to the point. "I crave ghostly counsel, holy father," she said.

"What is thy trouble, child?" the gentle voice asked. Its calm, yet alert tone of sympathy invited confidence. But what was the Lady Editha's trouble? This time she found it difficult to answer. "Father," she said at length, and with great simplicity, "heardst thou the sermon this morning? The Kingdom of Heaven is like unto a treasure hidden in a field. I want to buy that field, and I want to find the treasure."

It was spoken with the unconscious imperiousness of the heiress of the de Beauvilles who had never as yet lacked the wherewithal to buy that which she desired, yet it betrayed something of the child in its naivete, and Master Anker worshipped childhood.

"The price of the field is the last farthing," the old man said, in his gentle tones. "Whether thou hast four farthings or four thousand thou hast the wherewithal to buy it, so being that thou dost pay thy last one."

"Thou hast surely paid the last farthing, holy father," she whispered. "Tell me, what is it that thou hast found?"

She caught sight of the shaggy white head again. It was now framed in the narrow window, for he no longer feared the woman with the strained eyes and tightly-clasped hands. She could see his faded eyes gazing before him.

He opened his lips to speak. There was a curious kind of helplessness about him. He tried to find the necessary words but Master Anker was evidently not gifted with fluency of speech.

His client was kneeling on the stone, her clasped hands on the ledge. She gazed with seeking eyes into the shadows amongst which the anchor had dug up his treasure.

"But thou hast found it?" she questioned. He lowered his head. "Yea, child, after many years."

"Holy father," she cried, "tell me, what is this treasure?"

Then he answered,

"It is the love of Jesus." And he began softly to cry.

She waited for more, but Master Anker was no chartered instructor in the verities of the Faith. He had no grammar at his finger-tips, albeit that his theology was soundly in accord with the teaching of Holy Church. The Lady Editha waited in vain.

"Tell me what it means," she whispered, "the love of Jesus—to—those—to those who have found Him?"

She buried her face in her hands and prayed in a frenzy of desire that she might have light, that his words would enlighten her when they came.

But they never came. When she looked up he was still sitting, gazing before him with lips apart, precisely as he had been those long minutes ago. His wide-open eyes were fixed. A strange light appeared to be hovering about his head. Master Anker was powerless to give ghostly counsel to his client for he had passed into an ecstasy.

The Lady Editha lowered her awe-stricken eyes. The words of a hymn in her breviary had come rushing into her mind:—

> "Nec lingua valet dicere,
> Nec littera exprimere,
> Expertus potest credere,
> Quid sit Jesum diligere."—

It has been translated thus:—

> "But what to those who find? Ah that
> Nor tongue nor pen can show
> The love of Jesus what it is,
> None but His lov'd ones know."

What had she asked him to explain? That which the eye hath not seen, nor the ear heard. Nor shall it enter into the heart of man to conceive it, save that his heart be first emptied of all else beside.

"*Jesu, dulcis memoria!*" Upon the lute which was the soul of the Lady Editha de Beauville there had been struck one full chord containing in itself all music.

The great final banquet of the carnival took place on the Sunday evening. It was the last assembling of the guests who would tomorrow wend their way homeward.

Sir Aleric watched eagerly for the appearance of the Lady Editha. He had parted from her at mid-day, after Mass, and he had been left with that uncomfortable feeling that she was gazing over his head at something. He had not obtained access to her since. How would the preacher's words have affected her? Would there have supervened a desire to subdue the radiance of her personal charms. The preacher had shown such things to be vanity, and she had listened, oh how she had listened!

When the Lady Editha entered the banqueting hall on the baron's arm Sir Aleric's heart gave a mighty bound. She was more magnificent than ever! There was no diminution in the distinction of her bearing. The Lady Editha literally shone with jewels. Her sweeping robe was of heliotrope velvet embroidered with regal purple, her headdress a veiling of silver thread gathered into a golden fillet studded with amethysts. There was a bright pink flush, shell-like in its delicacy, on her cheek. Her eyes were a very deep blue, and soft, and very observant of all around her. They met Sir Aleric's with a sweet frankness of approval that sent him back into his heaven. It was a gay assembly. Chatter and laughter resounded on every side. The Queen of Beauty was the gayest among the gay. Her sparkling wit shot out at intervals to delight her neighbours. Sir Aleric's eyes scarcely left the radiant figure seated opposite to him at table. She was conversing once again with the old baron, and once again her near neighbours were neglecting their partners to listen. Her little shower of silvery laughter rang out ever and anon. The Lady Editha de Beauville was assessing her wealth to the utmost farthing.

The baron's eye had fallen on the King's chaplain who was seated some little way off. "A fine voice he hath," he commented. "I caught every word of the sermon this morning. A strange sermon it was, coming from such as he. It had more befitted a friar to speak so scornfully of the world's good things."

"Nay," the lady retorted, "but thou wrongest the good father. He spoke not with scorn of the world's goods. He spoke of them rather as possessing a mighty purchasing power. He showed the true value of all these things."

The old baron grunted. He laboured after the point.

"But tell me," the lady said, "What now is the value of a coin?"

"The value of what it buys," he answered, promptly enough.

"Yea, and that is the value of every possession," said she; "what the renouncing of it can buy of eternal goods."

Everyone had stopped talking to listen. The King's chaplain had caught the gist of their conversation and was listening with the others.

The old baron wagged his head. "Very fine in theory, no doubt," quoth he, "but who would put it into practice? How now, for the nonce. What eternal goods might one buy with a heritage like that of the de Beauvilles?"

"I should think me," the lady answered slowly, "that were all such wealth put together it might haply furnish the wherewithal to purchase an anchorhold."

The old man laughed. "Thou hast proved my point," he chuckled. "Pray, fair lady, dost thou intend to enter an anchorhold?"

A little laugh went round the listeners. They waited to see how the quick-witted lady would cover her retreat.

She looked at him smilingly. "That is my intention," she replied, rising calmly to her moment of triumph.

The old baron surveyed the glowing face, radiating its triumph with a quizzical though not unkindly smile. He had known her grandfather. This latest and thoroughly de Beauville vagary by no means took him by surprise.

"An' didst thou carry out that intention," he said, "I would give thee exactly a se'nnight in thy anchorhold."

The little laugh went round again. The company had not yet absorbed the situation. They were amused in a puzzled kind of way.

The Lady Editha assembled her forces. "That is a proposition, my lord," she answered quietly, "that it would take at least a se'nnight to contradict."

The other chuckled at the readiness of the repartee. "But why hast thou set thy choice on an anchorhold?" he asked, still bantering. "Methinks we could soon cure thee of it by sending thee round to pay a visit to Master Anker over against the church."

There was another laugh from the listeners. Many of them had been to visit Master Anker in his den, as a kind of zoological curiosity. Even in those days Master Anker's ideas of hygiene provoked comment.

"I have visited Master Anker," the lady said, in a low tone. Then she looked out bravely at the faces round. On most of them levity had given place to perplexity slightly mixed with disgust. The expression on the face of the Chaplain Royal was one of repulsion mingled with real concern.

The old baron continued: "And hath he caused thee to become enamoured of an anchorhold?"

The Lady Editha had not her answer ready this time. Her mind was handling something which could not be translated into the speech of these people. She glanced from face to face, and finally her eyes sought refuge in that of her true knight, Sir Aleric. He was deathly pale, and on his face was the same expression as on the others—sick repulsion. He was thinking of that same morning when she had shuddered at the mention of the anchorhold. What

strange spell had come over her since then? A sudden sense of isolation made itself felt. Her lip quivered, and the light that never
was on sea or land, shining in her eye, got itself mixed up in a tear
that was not allowed to fall. The Lady Editha de Beauville pulled
herself together to face a torture alien to her experience—to wit,
failure. She faced it as St. Catherine had faced her wheel, for the
Lady Editha intended to be another St. Catherine.

My lord the presiding baron, with the sixth sense of a perfect
host, felt that something was wrong. Probably Lollardry again. Or
perhaps the other ladies had been speaking pussy-cattily to the
Queen of Beauty (not, mark you, good reader, on account of their
sex, for God created pussy-cats male and female, like any other an-
imals, but because similarity of sex had given rise to rivalry). They
were probably getting back what they gave from the ready-witted
lady, but the baron felt that it was time to create a diversion. He
summoned Fiddlemee, who was, as before, seated within earshot
of the *tête-à-tête* that was arresting attention.

The jongleur sprang up into his seat and began to tune his instrument. His bright eyes glistened, as was always the case when
he was about to extemporize. He crossed his legs and waited for a
moment. Then he thumbed a little prelude and started to sing:—

> "Travellers from afar returning
> Have a traveller's tale to tell.
> They would teach us much concerning
> Things which never man befel—
> Travellers from afar returning
> Have a traveller's tale to tell.
>
> Travellers homing to their birth-place
> With a traveller's lore to teach
> Find a stranger on the hearth-place
> Understanding not their speech;
> Travellers homing to their birth-place
> Eke a strange new country reach.

Master Anker Maketh Music

Travellers from afar returning
Who a traveller's tale would tell,
For a kinsman vainly yearning,
Wander 'neath a strange, lone spell:
Travellers to the crowd returning
Must as solitaries dwell."

Sir Aleric's eyes were fixed not on the singer but on the woman opposite. He wondered if she were listening to the soft plaintive strains of the jongleur's haunting melody or to some music farther off. Her eyes were wide, like a child's, and wonderfully blue. It seemed to him that she was sitting there already a lady all alone— enclosed in her own vision. And he, Aleric, was kneeling outside gazing on her curtained window.

Chapter V

The Enclosing

IT WAS THE FAVOURITE occupation of such of the village folk as possessed the leisure to climb the cliff, on the edge of which stood the chantry chapel, to watch Peter the mason, the Lady Prioress's man, and his assistants at work.

The chantry chapel of St. Catherine stood overlooking the tiny cove where the fisher-folk foregathered in rude hovels built on the sea-shore, and ministered to the spiritual needs of the latter whilst keeping in remembrance before heaven the soul of the pious knight by whom it had been founded. It supported a chaplain who said his Mass there daily but domiciled at the rectory in the inlying village with Sir Simon the parson, to whom he acted as curate, as the chantry chaplain was expected to do. It was a geographical peculiarity of the neighbourhood that the great white highway that conducted merchants and pilgrims to the east Anglian metropolis took a rather invidious swerve at this point which carried it to the foot of the ascent on which the chantry chapel stood, whilst bearing it away from the village and the parish church by which St. Catherine's was ecclesiastically mothered, thus leaving the villagers in a kind of backwater which they ill-appreciated.

Perched up on the cliff, on the wind-swept but fertile meadowland, was also the convent, girded by outlying buildings where a community of conventual dependents carried on a flourishing farming industry under the remarkably able direction of Master John Matt, the Lady Prioress's bailiff. The convent was situated about a quarter of a mile from the chapel. Its present flourishing condition was of but recent growth. Little more than a year ago it had been a moribund foundation with a small community of semi-starved religious. At that juncture there had come along a noble and wealthy lady who wished to enter religion, and it was with her wealth that the broad acres adjoining the convent land had been purchased and put under cultivation. It was said that the new novice herself had schemed out the whole plan by which a flourishing little industrial community was established in the cottages erected under the eye of Master John Matt. Some even declared that the great lady had herself designed the comfortable little habitations, and thought out the elaborate scheme for draining the swampy land and making the air round the convent sweet and savoury. The convent itself had been practically rebuilt and remodelled. Its fame as a model religious house had got abroad and many other members of noble families had joined the community, or else been sent there to complete their education.

In both the villages the various building operations had provoked much interest, and many had trudged the intervening mile or climbed the cliff as the case might be, to watch the masons and locksmiths at their work. The present operations, however, were of a far more thrilling and curiosity-provoking nature. The Lady Prioress's workmen were engaged in erecting an anchorhold up against the chapel of St. Catherine, and it was rumoured that it was the great lady herself—the one whose wealth and wit had effected the changes at the convent, who was to occupy the cell. As a natural consequence enormous interest was displayed in the new erection. It was a sturdy stone building, built upon an arched undercroft, evidently intended to stand the ravages of time. In design it displayed the same ingenuity that had been expended on the cottages. The anchorage was a perfect model in its way of what an anchorage should be. The "parlour" window was there. It was a gracefully designed mullioned window, becomingly narrow in its

dimensions, glazed with horn on the upper part and curtained below, and in addition to this there were lights, sufficiently high in the
wall to ensure privacy, so that the cell should possess a sufficiency
of daylight. Its architect had thought the thing out thoroughly in
every respect. It was an austere and withal a dignified retreat for
the holy lady who would be known in the future by the name of
"Dame Catherine." There was a door at the back of the anchorage of
stout oak, and the spectators greatly enjoyed the thrill of watching
Jack the locksmith fix the huge impregnable lock in its place. But
this thrill was enormously accentuated when it was discovered that
the door would but lead to an outer apartment where the anchoress's attendants would remain whilst preparing her meal or kindling a fire. There was a window looking into the cell beyond, but
no door, for the archway in the partitioning wall as it appeared to
those who paid visits of inspection to the work in progress, would
be walled up by Peter the mason in solemn wise after my lord the
bishop had conducted the anchoress to her enclosure, and no foot
would pass over the threshold of the anchorhold itself. The incluse
would dwell solitary in her cell, its parlour window, duly curtained
when visitors came to receive ghostly counsel, looking upon the
world which she had left for ever, and another, piercing the wall of
the church so as to command a view of the high altar, looking on
the world opened up to the gaze of the anchorite. It was a daring
hark back to an ideal of sanctity that already belonged to the past.

It had been difficult to obtain the bishop's permission for the
actual immuring. This austere form of enclosing had always been
reserved for those only who displayed extraordinary signs of sanctity, and the locked door, sealed with the bishop's seal, was the utmost accorded to the religious aspirations of the would-be recluse
at that period. The present anchoress, however, had contrived to
get her own way. The bishop had yielded, and was even coming
himself to perform the ceremony of enclosing. The candidate had
obediently served her noviceship in a religious house, and stoutly

withstood the clamour of the community to make her their prioress, adhering to her original intention with a constancy that could not be shaken. The inmate of the anchorage was to be known simply as "Mother Catherine," the name of the saint to whose church she was attached. The suppression of her worldly name left room for much speculation. Some said it was Lady Editha de Beauville, others that it was none less than a royal princess who was to bury herself in the anchorhold in the fisherman's churchyard. "Dame Catherine" covered all these surmises, and moreover cast a glamour of romance over the figure of the anchoress-elect.

The day appointed for the enclosing of the anchoress was observed as a high festival by the villagers. Such an occasion was sufficient to justify a suspension of the ordinary routine of life. Many hours before that fixed for the ceremony the entire population had turned out of the village and streamed along the road leading to the cliff-side. The fisher-folk had likewise climbed up in a body to witness the ceremony.

They were somewhat awestruck at the thought of this holy lady in their midst. In a sense she would belong to them, since she had elected to dwell up against their chapel, the light from whose beacon tower guided them to safety amidst the rocks and quicksands which were the chief perils of the high seas upon which they plied their calling, but on the whole they were inclined to regard the newcomer as belonging to the world that passed near enough to the cliff-side chapel on the swerving high road. The vicinity of the latter had, indeed, helped in the selection of the spot, for one of the features of the anchorhold was that it should lie near the ways where the world passed to and fro.

Sir Simon, the parson, was there in his canonicals, with the chaplain of St. Catherine's, similarly vested. They waited at the chapel door whilst the crowd of sightseers lined the path along which the bishop and his attendants would conduct the anchoress to her life-long dwelling. The chapel itself was filled to overflowing, for there the main part of the ceremony would be performed, and there the bishop would address the aspirant to heroic sanctity on the subject of her vows. Certainly such a holiday didn't often come in the way of ordinary village folk.

The churchyard possessed the aspect of some famous shrine around which a kind of perpetual religious fair is held. No doubt in the future it would become a place of pilgrimage, for she who sought enclosure was said to be a woman possessing wonderful gifts of understanding and of speech whereby she might enlighten those who sought her window. Folks from a distance had brought their bread and cheese with them and were picnicking, very much at their ease. New arrivals trailed in a never-ceasing file past the anchorage, with its open door yielding a glimpse of the stack of piled-up bricks within awaiting the hand of Peter the mason, to consummate the ceremony of the enclosing. Some enterprising pedlars had gone so far as to take advantage of the occasion and were driving a trade in objects of piety and other home-made souvenirs of the historic occasion. A few wandering minstrels had even arrived on the scene and had been enlivening the hours of waiting with their songs.

One of these was a bright-eyed fellow with a thin, dark face. He had arrived in good time and had made a minute inspection of the anchorage, accompanied by his dog, Flipkin. Fiddlemee's lute was in his bag, slung across his back. He made no attempt to put it to use to earn a dinner as the others were doing. He finally sat himself on the grass at a little distance, hugging his knees and whispering to his dog, as he had done on a former occasion.

The hour fixed for the enclosing was drawing near. The seated folk rose and pressed towards the path facing the door of the anchorage, which was the most coveted position, commanding as it did a view of the dramatic climax—the passing of the recluse over the threshold which she would never recross. All awaited the procession from the convent which was even now wending its way across the meadows.

The Enclosing

The arrival of my lord the bishop with his retinue of chaplains and lay attendants from the convent where he had been receiving hospitality was the first excitement. He was received at the door of the chapel by Sir Simon and his coadjutor and conducted to the sanctuary where his improvised throne, draped in red velvet, awaited him, faced by the uncushioned prie-dieu placed for the use of the *includenda*, or intending incluse.

Meanwhile the other procession approached. It consisted of the convent chaplain, an elderly Franciscan of austere habit, with two acolytes bearing lighted tapers, followed by the extern sisters of the convent—those who were not bound by the rule of enclosure which was very strictly adhered to under the present *régime*. Between them came the figure of the heroine of the occasion. She was dressed in white, and veiled. Behind, again, at a respectful distance, there walked Peter the mason, attended by his two apprentices, all three garbed in fresh white smocks, and Jack the locksmith in a new leather jerkin—the world was not going to be allowed to forget how completely it was to be shut out by her for whose ghostly protection the anchorhold had been raised, secure against all would-be intruders.

The spectators craned their necks to gain sight of the strange procession. There was one of these, however, who had no need to do so for he stood head and shoulders above the others. He was a magnificent man, magnificently dressed, albeit after the manner of those who go to do battle for the cross. His fine, clear-cut features were set in a mask-like expression which yet more effectively betrayed the pain which it was intended to conceal. Sir Aleric's sea-blue eyes were strained towards the centre of the procession. Even from that distance the indescribable charm of the lissome, slender figure, so characteristic of its owner, served to bring before his vision the entire woman. Her elusive beauty, the enchantment of the rich, low-toned voice—the silver ripple of her laughter—the soft shimmer on her eyes when some musician, as the mad jongleur had expressed it, made fresh music on her soul. She came back to him with overwhelming completeness as he outlined the distant figure, with its grace, and the tender dignity, that made her "Queen Mab" withal. Those nearby heard the deep drawn breath which was a suppressed groan of anguish.

The procession came nearer. It passed the spot upon which he was standing. The veiled head was bent, as was seemly. Her meekness was so exquisite, her reverence so faithfully expressed by the delicately responsive material covering of the soul of the Lady Editha.

She passed with her escort into the chapel where the bishop was about to sing Mass. On the high altar was set the lighted candle which she would hold during the celebration of the holy mysteries.

The bishop duly delivered his address. It ran on definite and stereotyped lines. The aspirant was reminded that it was in order to escape the dangers and pitfalls of the world that she sought this seclusion. She was bidden to believe this that she might escape the sin of vainglory. Humiliating words which were, however, shorn of their sting by the fact that they were prescribed to be used on all such occasions. The intending recluse—the *includenda* of the *rituale*, knelt in her place and listened with bent head. The tall knight stood just within the doorway, his hands clenched and his fingernails pressed into his flesh. He glanced down at the scarlet cross embroidered on his shoulder. Yea, forsooth, he was going to battle, and she was running away. Hiding from the alleged perils of the world, from the common enemy, in this fastness. She with her gifts and graces wherewith to trade and traffic. Oh, the colossal pity of it!

Mass over, the procession was reformed. The singing boys who headed it started to sing the great mystical hymn of deliverance, the psalm, "When Israel came out of Egypt," which is the "new canticle" of every soul which makes the great renunciation. Once again Sir Aleric clutched his sword-hilt. Thus their ways had parted—at the moment of union. His vocation to face the battle, hers to evade it. And she so strong, so individual, so fearless, so bountifully equipped. Her personality was as one in ten thousand. He hurried out and pressed his way grimly to the spot which commanded the door of the anchorage and the path thither. The singing boys approached on the latter—then the clergy and the chaplains, followed by the bishop in his imposing pontificals. The figure in white walked behind them.

The lady carried her lighted taper, and this time her head was uplifted—thrown back in eagerness rather than triumph, although the latter was there, shining in the urgent eyes. The knight saw her face for a moment. It was a trifle thinner than of yore, even more shell-like in its delicacy after the year of austerities, and more than ever dominated by the great shining eyes relentlessly fixed on the things from which the body shrinks and recoils. What a tyrant spirit it was that inhabited that frail form! Was it this ruthless domination that gave its underlying pathos to that delicate-featured countenance, and the slender frame which was, after all, rather below medium height? He felt a clutch at his heart. Oh, that he might play knight errant and save her from herself—the tender woman in whose eyes the tears had stood when he spoke to her of his worship—who had laughed with very joy at the delicacy of a compliment conveyed through a witticism—this woman who *loved* to be loved!

She had reached her abiding-place. Once more her head was bent as she approached its threshold. The onlookers stood spellbound by the glimpse of the eager uplifted countenance. Sir Aleric found himself noting that the very folds of her roughly-cut garment had placed themselves in perfect lines as they fell about her, in that last glimpse he got of the disappearing figure as the *includenda* took the step which made her *inclusa*—one "serving the Divine Goodness in the order of Anchorites, by the grace of God and the counsel of Holy Church."

So she passed in, with unfaltering footstep. The bishop followed her. He would be sprinkling her with holy water as she lay prone on the floor of her cell. He would be placing a little earth upon her, signifying her burial. The world had lost the Lady Editha de Beauville. And now Peter the mason was swiftly building up a partition wall of brick. A single layer—a barrier, symbolical rather than actual. One that could be as swiftly removed when the anchoress had passed from hence by another way. In a very few minutes it was accomplished, whilst she lay there prostrate on the floor. The bishop emerged from the anchorage with Peter and his assistant. The enclosing of the anchoress was accomplished.

Jack the locksmith stepped forward and inserted the big key in the new lock. It turned with a grating sound. The Lady Editha de Beauville had in sooth determined that no intruder should break through the bolts and bars and brick walls with which she had guarded the field in which she was to seek the hidden treasure.

A chill silence fell on the spectators. Some felt that they had no wish to be present at another enclosing. Then there burst upon the air a shout of music—the Church's cry of jubilation—"*Te Deum Laudamus!*" The crowd thinned off with considerable rapidity, their departure accelerated by the stewards of the occasion, lest they should loiter round the new habitation of the *incluse* lady and disturb her devotions by the sound of their voices.

Sir Aleric moved away with the rest. He stood and regarded the anchorage from afar off. Someone at his side was doing the same. He turned round quickly and recognised Fiddlemee, the mad jongleur. It was another association with the great week of his life. Fiddlemee and he had been good friends. The other regarded him, surveying his cloak with its indicative cross.

"So thou ridest to the Holy War, Sir Knight," he observed. "Thou hast found thy vocation since we last met, as also hath the lady yonder. Methinks she was the first to find hers, for all that thou hast donned the crutch before she entered into her own."

His glance was as shrewd as ever. "'Tis a mighty vocation to fight in the Holy War," he went on, "as doubtless she herself told thee."

The other's countenance set itself grimly. "And yet," quoth he, "she herself sits shut away from the battle, a solitary, where there is no foe to fight."

"No foe to fight!" the other echoed. "Beshrew me but thy highness must be jesting! The holy Dame Catherine goes up thither to fight the Lady Editha de Beauville, and at closer quarters than thou wilt ever get to the Turk, or so I pray God, Sir Knight. And," he added, piously, "may Holy Michael be with her in the day of battle."

Chapter VI

The Loose Brick

I CAN'T PRETEND to say how it was that the chronicle of Dame Catherine, the holy anchoress, came to include the following episode. Certain it is that the incident here recorded was not divulged by Sister Felicity. Not all the torments suffered by her holy namesake and those of her companions, all rolled into one, could have dragged the story from Felicity. It may have been that the anchoress told it herself to the chaplain who afterwards became her chronicler, after she had attained to the third degree of humility, and the latter may have found it wise to include it in the chronicle which purports to represent Dame Catherine as she was. At any rate this is the story:—Sister Perpetua and Sister Felicity were so named from the sufficiently obvious reason that they entered religion together on the 6th of March, the Feast of the valiant African martyrs. They were both extern sisters, exempt from the rule of enclosure which had been re-established and strictly enforced by the present Prioress at the time of her election. This was about the time of the coming of the Lady Editha de Beauville to undergo her novitiate in preparation for the recluse life which she had in view. The general stiffening up of the convent's spiritual *régime* had been concurrent with the material improvements that had made it famous round the country-side, and it was said that the same mind was behind both, and behind the Lady Prioress as well.

When at the end of her year of probation the Lady Editha passed from her cell in the cloister to the more austere seclusion of the anchorhold built up against the chapel of St. Catherine, from which she would henceforth take her name, Perpetua and Felicity were told off to act as serving-maids to the anchoress. They had charge of the key of the anchorhold, and it was their duty to carry thither the necessities of this life and pass them through the window of the outer cell to the enclosed lady. Felicity and Perpetua were an oddly assorted pair. Perpetua was thin and pensive-looking. She observed the custody of the eyes with edifying strictness, being a holy soul, though one who took her religious life without the mirthfulness which we have it on the authority of the mediæval mystics is proper to the religious state. No one had ever accused Perpetua of levity, and if, on the other hand, no one had ever dubbed her a pessimist it was simply because the word, though not the disease, was not invented in her day.

Felicity, on the contrary, was stout and smiling—buxom in the sense of the word as used in those days; that is to say, of an easy and kindly disposition, one not to be easily set up against the world she lived in. Felicity kept her rule in the course of nature, save in the matter of the custody of the eyes. Felicity might have had eyes all round her head for the number of things that she managed to observe. She certainly was an indifferent custodian of the two that gave its comeliness to the big, rosy, snub-nosed countenance. Felicity invariably saw the cheerful side of life, in religion and out of it. She and Perpetua had waited upon the Lady Editha in her retirement, and Felicity had thoroughly enjoyed the task, for the holy lady, for all her holiness, was not above being lured into passing a gay remark with her waiting-maid, and moreover she was a remarkably winsome sight in her demure black robe, with her Queen Mab countenance framed in the soft white wimple. Felicity loved pretty sights. Perpetua always waited on the recluse-elect with correctly downcast eyes. Not so, Felicity. Oh, dear, no!

Perpetua and Felicity occasionally discussed their lady at times when talking was permitted. Perpetua invariably looked grave and shook her head. She entertained serious doubts as to the future of the would-be recluse.

The anchorage was rising, stone by stone, and the lady was following its progress with eager interest, but Perpetua shook her head. The Lady Editha would tire of her stern resolution long before Peter the mason and his apprentices had finished their task. Perpetua's grandfather had been a villein owning his five acres on the de Beauville estate and he knew their kind. No de Beauville had ever been known to adhere for any length of time to any one line of action. Weariness and disgust would overcome the recluse lady ere it was time to seek the stricter enclosing of the anchorhold.

Felicity thought otherwise. Being an optimist she vowed her fealty to success, and on principle, so to speak, upheld the thesis that the Lady Editha would consummate her heart's desire. In vain might Perpetua shake her head and grimly contend that it was the heart's desire that was unstable in the de Beauville temperament, so accurately comprehended by her grandfather the villein. Felicity stuck to her opinion, and scored a triumph when the day approached which was to witness the enclosing of the anchoress.

But Perpetua still shook her head, and with unflinching pessimism opined that the enclosing would be of but a temporary nature. The Lady Editha had been kept going by the interest of seeing her ingenious housing design carried out by the builders. Once the novelty of enclosure was over, the inevitable change in her ideas concerning her true vocation would occur.

Doleful doubting is an insidious thing with which to be brought into incessant contact. It might have been that even Felicity began to have doubts as to the ultimate success of the experiment—but however that may have been the case, certain it is that, as has been said, all the torments suffered by her patron saint could not have wrung an admission from Felicity to that effect. She and Perpetua visited the newly-enclosed lady and found her full of sweetness and contentment and good cheer. There could be no doubt so far that the anchoress was radiantly happy. Perpetua sighed heavily at the ominous portent. "'Tis the flash in the pan," she said, sadly, "a sure sign that it won't last. 'Tis not like going into religion properly, this life that she hath taken upon herself. 'Twere like the de Beauvilles to make such strange choice—for the nonce."

"She seemeth very happy," Felicity answered, thinking on the radiant face seen through the uncurtained inner window by the privileged waiting-maids.

"'Tis the de Beauville way," Perpetua replied. "My grandfather hath said that 'twas the staying power that was lacking; they ever loved the new thing because it was new, and nought on earth ever remaineth new, nor goods nor friends, nor anything."

"Then the more reason," Felicity retorted, "for seeking the things which are in Heaven, for methinks that they remain ever new."

It was not so bad a repartee.

"Yea verily," Perpetua responded heavily. Then she cheered up a little. "But yon anchorhold is on earth, not in heaven," she answered. She ran her eye over the heaving sod of the graveyard, and in the jargon of a later day Perpetua might be said to have been "bucked" by the contemplation of the tombs of the dead.

It must be admitted that her attitude affected Felicity's optimistic belief in the staying power of the recluse lady to the extent of making her more or less on the look-out for symptoms of the de Beauville malady. A de Beauville between four walls was a thing never heard of, the villein's granddaughter declared. "She will have the walls down with her naked hands, an so it were denied to let her forth, when her mood changeth."

It was this observation that caused Felicity to view with something akin to disquiet an incident, slight in itself, which occurred a little later. It happened one day that when she and Perpetua entered the outer cell the curtain was carefully drawn over the inner window. Instead of greeting her waiting-maids, as was her wont, the anchoress merely thrust her hands through the aperture to receive the victuals which her attendants had brought for her consumption. This in itself was not extraordinary. The holy lady was not of necessity accessible to her maids any more than to the outside world. The sinister point about the incident was this. Felicity's eagle eye was swift to note that on the knuckles of the hands with which the recluse received her food the skin was broken and seared. She prayed devoutly that her companion might not have noted the circumstance, and on the following day, the curtain being still drawn, she took good care that it was she and not Perpetua who passed the Anchoress her necessities. The inmate of the anchorhold had now been enclosed for over six months and all had gone well. Even Perpetua's indomitable pessimism had received a set-back. During that time the anchoress had made periodical "retreats" from the ken of her serving-maids, but Felicity felt a qualm in her heart as to the real meaning of the present seclusion. "Dame Catherine" certainly had not been quite herself for some days past. Felicity wondered what exactly was happening behind the drawn curtain. Perpetua didn't wonder, she simply waited, forgetting even to shake her head and prophesy.

Felicity ached to say a word to the enclosed lady but the drawn curtain strictly forbade such a liberty. "She's come to the end of her tether," Perpetua said, as they approached the anchorage next day, "and if the bishop doth not let her hence she'll be like to have the walls down with her own hands."

Felicity thought again of the broken skin on the knuckles of the anchoress's hands and snatched the basket of provisions from her companion. "Thou hast the key," quoth she, "I'll see to this."

As they approached the anchorhold something impelled Felicity to take over the key as well as the basket. When she entered the door she saw at once that something had happened. She had barely time to set down her burden and cross the cell before Perpetua followed her in. The latter found Felicity standing with her back to the inner wall, near the still curtained window. She remained there, watching Perpetua set down her bundle of faggots and made no offer to assist in the lighting of the fire. Perpetua set about the task meekly. It was neither fair nor just that she should do it all by herself, but Perpetua remembered that a true religious has no truck with rights and dues, and her dozen years of religious profession had in no wise diminished her holy ardour. She, at any rate, was not afflicted with the defect of the de Beauvilles. She remembered this and accepted the situation as meekly as though in the first year of her novitiate.

Felicity stood and watched her lay the faggots on the hearth. "There was a man coming along, methought, towards the parlour window," she observed. "It might be well if he were told that the holy Mother is in seclusion? If thou wouldst like to go and see I will kindle the fire."

Perpetua demurred. The anchoress's visitors were the subject of much discussion at the convent. Curiosity impelled Perpetua to accept the suggestion, but she immediately recognised it as a temptation—also as a means of mortification. "Nay," she said, "why should I go? He can but go away again." She did not suggest that Felicity should go herself. Felicity needed to mortify the concupiscence of the eyes far more than she did.

She applied herself to arranging the faggots.

Felicity continued to regard her companion's activity without budging. "There is a drop of milk," she remarked after a moment or two, "at the bottom of the jug. Pusskin might like to have it, if she be about. She generally sleepeth under the parlour window. I've a mind to go and seek her, for it's an act of charity though it be to a dumb beast. But perhaps it be hardly worth the trouble, the visitor, if he cometh, will be driving her away."

"Nay, I will go," Perpetua said, "if it troubleth thee. It would indeed be an act of mercy to the dumb beast." She left the faggots and slipped out quickly through the open door.

Felicity scarcely allowed herself time to chuckle. She just managed a *Deo Gratias* as she stepped aside from where she was standing and turned quickly round. Where her broad shoulders had been there was a gap in the wall; and on the floor where she had been standing there lay a brick. Peter the mason had borne in mind the fact that his work was not to be of a permanent character and had used little mortar to cement his bricks.

Quick as thought Felicity picked up the brick and thrust it back into its place. It was done in a second and the danger was averted. The anchoress was saved. Then, forgetful of that which is done, or not done, in an anchorage, she proceeded to sit herself down by the window. She lifted up one side of the curtain and inserted in its place her broad, beaming countenance, indicating with great simplicity that all was well.

Regardless of everything except the mother feeling that welled up in her heart, Felicity thrust her head into the sanctum sanctorum and addressed the inmate in the vernacular.

"It's all right, my dearie," Felicity said. "Perpetua be gone round to look for the cat and she's not seen nothing. *I stood on it*—in front of the gap. Don't 'ee fear, my pretty dearie, it's all right."

Felicity's "it's all right" could be taken to include a reticence which could not be shaken by the application of the united torments of Perpetua, Felicitas and their five companions.

When Perpetua returned she found a repentant Felicity very busily engaged in attending to the faggots. "I couldn't find Pusskin," she said, "and there was no visitor."

"Visitor?" Felicity said, demurely. "Oh, yes, I did say something about a visitor, didn't I?"

The information anent Pusskin had no interest for her, from the fact that she had previously met the anchoress's lady tabby three meadows off heading for the convent.

When they returned on the following day a change had taken place. The curtain was withdrawn and a very sweet, serene and peaceful incluse lady was waiting on their ministrations.

Even Perpetua was deeply impressed. Her cassandra tongue was silenced. "She seemeth very well content, after all," she observed, as they walked home. "Yet, methinks she hath been through a struggle, for she hath a worn and weary look about her."

"Yea, but she hath conquered," Felicity answered, triumphantly. "God hath sent His angel to drive away her foe, since He doth intend that she shall endure to stay there, even though she be a de Beauville," she added, sturdily. "And," added she, "I should like well to have been the angel who had the doing of it—the pretty dear!"

Dear Felicity! Verily one would be glad to be the angel who in Heaven will have the joy of telling thee who the angel was who drove the dark fiend of desolation from the very human heart of Dame Catherine, the holy anchoress.

Chapter VII

"*My Lady Nobody?*"

IDDLEMEE THE JONGLEUR was riding northward in the retinue of His Grace the Duke. He was riding by the latter's side so as to point out the places of interest by the way and keep His Grace amused by his conversation. They had reached the point where the high road looped round, giving the cold shoulder to the village through which, normally speaking, it should have passed. Fiddlemee explained how a long-standing dispute as to the right of way had caused this curious digression in the King's highway, lengthening the journey north by about three-quarters of a mile. He also pointed out that the swerve in the road would bring them close up to the cliff-side upon which stood the beacon chapel, to which an anchorhold was attached.

"'Tis a passing holy woman, the anchoress who inhabits there," Fiddlemee observed. "Rumour saith that she was once a very great lady in the world. They say her name was the Lady Editha de Beauville, and that she was heiress to the de Beauville estates."

His Grace the Duke sat up straight in his saddle. He was prodigious interested. "Art thou sure?" he cried. "I knew the Lady Editha well. A mighty remarkable woman she was, with a mind like a man's and a pretty wit withal. A ravishing, sylph-like creature to look upon. All the world was in love with her; and yet, beshrew me; all the world couldn't say why. They did say that she had gone into religion, but 'od body, an anchorhold! Thou art surely mistaken?"

"The anchoress calleth herself Dame Catherine, after the chapel," Fiddlemee replied, "but I have always heard that it is the Lady Editha de Beauville in very sooth. She hath a great following at her parlour window, hath 'Dame Catherine.' All sorts of holy and learned folks stop to pay her court if they chance to be journeying this way."

His Grace gazed up with considerable curiosity at the grey, reed-thatched excrescence. "If it indeed be the Lady Editha," he remarked, "I would fain go up and pay court to her myself, for it were the most winsome woman that I ever cast eyes on, the Lady Editha."

"Thou wouldst not cast eyes on her now," Fiddlemee answered drily. "Her curtain is ever drawn before her parlour window, and she speaketh but to give ghostly counsel."

The duke's curiosity was more than ever tickled. There was a piquancy about the whole thing that afforded quite a fresh sensation to his *blasé* soul. "Methinks I will go up and seek ghostly counsel," he remarked, imitating Fiddlemee's dry tone. "Nay," he corrected himself. "Go thou up first whilst I rest at the inn and find out if it indeed be the Lady Editha, for it be mighty hard to credit that such a one as she be indeed immured in yonder hole since—how long might it be?"

"About five years, an' so they tell me," Fiddlemee replied.

His Grace the Duke muttered an oath of the period expressive of his amazement. He was now bubbling over with curiosity and eagerness to revive his acquaintance with the Lady Editha under the present quaint circumstances. He hurried Fiddlemee off on his mission there and then, riding on with his retinue towards the inn.

Fiddlemee dismounted and proceeded on his errand on foot, as was necessary. He approached the anchorage respectfully and knelt himself down in a humble posture before the parlour window, after he had warned the anchoress of his approach by tinkling the little bell attached to the hedge which screened the path leading to the anchorage.

A gentle *Dominus tecum* told him that the anchoress was in attendance.

"Holy Mother," Fiddlemee said, delivering his message with all due promptness, "my master His Grace the Duke of —— passeth this way and wisheth to pay his respects to one whom he formerly knew as the Lady Editha de Beauville that he may receive ghostly counsel for his soul."

"Since when hath His Grace the Duke of —— come by the habit of seeking ghostly counsel?" the lady anchoress enquired, and her tones were even drier than those either of Fiddlemee or the duke had been. It was most assuredly the Lady Editha's own, that imperious note and the touch of sarcasm which had spiced her wit in the old days.

"Since that he hath heard that the holy Dame Catherine is ready to give it," Fiddlemee replied, promptly. "My master doth not solicit ghostly counsel of the Lady Editha but of 'Dame Catherine,' the lady named after the saint of this chapel."

"Tell thy master," the voice replied—Fiddlemee's imagination supplied the flashing eye and curling lip—"Tell thy master that Dame Catherine bids him know that she hath no traffic with the satellites of the Lady Editha de Beauville—she takes no cognisance of the Lady Editha."

"And yet she doth mightily resemble her," the jongleur replied.

"I have no cognisance of her," Dame Catherine repeated coldly.

"The Lady Editha, most holy Mother," the other said, "was a lady that was full scornful of small ideals and mean ambitions. She possessed much wealth and did invest it in the buying of a field wherein lay hidden a treasure." (There was a sound of a slight movement within.) "That is, methinks she did indeed invest all and buy the whole field. She was a shrewd woman, and she knew that not to buy the whole field would have been folly, and belike much waste of purchase money, for the hidden treasure might have lain in the rood that did not become hers."

He paused and waited.

"Who art thou?" the voice of the anchoress asked. It was no longer scornful, but full of fear and disquiet. "Art thou a priest or a sorcerer?"

"I am neither, but only Fiddlemee the jongleur," was the reply. "But, holy Mother, if ever the Lady Editha comes thy way bid her have a care that she verily hath purchased the whole field, or all her purchasing may be in vain."

"How should she know that she hath indeed purchased the whole field?" the anchoress asked. Her voice had become very quiet and meek.

"She should know whether she hath paid the full price," Fiddlemee replied.

"And what is the full price?"

"Everything, I trow me," was the answer. "The Lady Editha would have to part with all her belongings, including herself."

"But I have told thee that I have no traffic with the Lady Editha." The words came in the petulant tones of the spoiled child of the house of de Beauville.

"Nay, nay, but she speaketh now," Fiddlemee retorted. "She hath sent a message to my master, His Grace, that no Dame Catherine that was verily born so and not named after the chapel would have dared to send. In sooth he will accept it meekly enough— from 'My Lady Nobody.'"

The speaker's eyes were fixed upon the white cross in the centre of the black curtain behind which the listener sat. His face was ashen pale. His hands clasped the ledge as he waited for the reply.

It came at last, in low tones.

"I thank thee, good fellow, for thy words. Go and tell thy master what thou thinkest best and most seemly. And now I pray thee leave me to my prayers." There was a little break in the full tones. Fiddlemee had a vision of a child about to cry. Something twisted his heart-strings round and round. The tears came into his eyes, and poured down his cheeks. *"Deo gratias!"* he whispered, and crossed himself.

His Grace the Duke was speechless with chagrin when Fiddlemee, with a crestfallen air, delivered his message. "The holy lady called Dame Catherine hath no cognisance of the Lady Editha de Beauville."

"I have a mind to have thee whipped for an idle gossiping knave," the Duke declared. "See, the time that thou hast caused me to waste with thy foolish tales. 'Tis well that I sent thee first to enquire. A pretty figure I should have cut dancing after some convent wench with a maggot in her brain. One might have known that had the Lady Editha tried such a game—and she was wilful enough to try anything that seized her fancy, she would have stayed perhaps a week, and then had enough of playing the anchoress."

"It may be that the Lady Editha is dead," Fiddlemee suggested. But his lord was too sulky to continue the conversation, and the jongleur found himself in possession of some time for thought, a luxury of which he was swift to take advantage.

An hour later the Duke recovered his good humour. He made his silent companion a sporting offer of a penny for his thoughts.

"I was thinking," Fiddlemee said, "that the Lady Editha de Beauville *is* dead."

The Duke revenged himself later on his inaccurate retainer. The latter was summoned that evening, after their return to the castle, to sing a song to Her Grace the Duchess in her bower. The cycle of love-ditties demanded by the occasion finished, His Grace condescended to twit the jongleur on the sore subject. "How now," he cried, facetiously, "let us have a change. Sing us a song about a holy anchoress."

The singer ran his finger over his strings. He tightened a peg, listening to ensure a perfect concord of tones. Then he began:—

"My Lady Nobody?"

"I without and thou within,
Can the angels call us kin
Howsoe'er I pause to bide
At thy casement's outer side?

Two small windows hath the cell
Where thou dost as ankret dwell,
Through the one my path thou trace,
One gives on the holy place.

Two small windows must there be;
Through the one thou giv'st to me—
Me with pilgrim's sandal shod,
Through the other take from God.

Fain I'd pass the threshold o'er
Held thine anchorhold a door,
But thy cell is walled about,
Thou within and I without.

Vainly to the bars I press
Peeping at the anchoress,
But her gift alone I ken
Who, receiving, gives again.

I without and thou within,
Right of entry did I win
Ankret still, thou'd hide from sight
In His countenance's light."

The Duke's little son and heir broke the silence that followed the last note of the simple yet arresting melody. "That is much the prettiest song of all," he said to his governess, "but why was the funny man crying?"

Chapter VIII

Nicholas the Chaplain

IR SIMON, THE PARSON, was initiating his new curate, the chantry priest of St. Catherine's chapel of ease, into his new duties. Nicholas the chaplain was an Oxford scholar, fresh from that hot-bed of ideas and impulses, things looked upon askance by Sir Simon, and Sir Simon's cure of souls was a social backwater, remote from the stream of life. The main road, along which all the northward traffic passed, curved and gave the village a wide berth, choosing, as it were, to wend its way past the steep, sudden ascent on whose summit stood the chantry chapel with its beacon tower giving light and warning to those at sea. The pious founder of the chapel had had the souls as well as the bodies of the seafaring men in mind, hence the bequest for a priest who should say Mass daily for those in danger on sea or land. The chantry chaplain was appointed by the bishop. He domiciled at the rectory and was expected to be at the rector's disposal for parochial purposes, virtually serving as curate.

The new chaplain had been but recently priested. He was a pleasant-looking young man, with an eager, boyish way about him, plainly out to set the world to rights and keenly alive to all those things to which Sir Simon was most successfully mortified—to wit, the burning questions of the day. No question had ever succeeded in burning the soul of Sir Simon, he was constitutionally impervious even to a singeing process. He perceived readily enough that the young man whom the bishop had consigned to his supervision had a hot head, and sufficient energy of action to make him a fidgetty element in the sheepfold. Still, properly controlled, he would have his uses. The poor children needed schoolmastering, and some chantry chaplains would fight shy of this extraneous office. Young Sir Nicholas had accepted it with the utmost goodwill, so the good parson was satisfied, upon the whole, with the bishop's choice. He appeared to be a discreet enough young man, wearing his coat cut the right length and closed in front although he frankly indulged in the dental laugh disparaged by the rule laid down for the deportment of those in Holy Orders. Moreover, he showed no signs of flouting the ordinances of Holy Church as did the followers of the Lollard trend of thought. Sir Simon, having duly welcomed and fed the new arrival, for he possessed the priestly virtue of hospitality in a high degree, had walked him across the meadows to the scene of his future ministrations. They had arrived at the big yew tree at the foot of the sloping God's acre, strewn with the graves of the fisher-folk, whose burial-place it was.

Young Nicholas the chaplain stood and gazed with a sinking in his heart on the little isolated chapel. His appointment to this rural backwater had been a severe shock to his expectations. He had dreamt of a cure in some centre of light and learning, and movement—movement possessing sufficient velocity to form a counter-campaign to that carried on with such mischievous zeal by the "poor priests," and the heretical band of so-called friars who made spiritual war on the established church and the existing mendicant orders. The spiritual difficulties of his age were ever present in the mind of Nicholas. Sheep there were indeed who were not being fed. Scandals existed. His generation had fallen upon evil times, and many of those who held the Church's treasure held it buried away in a napkin, or so it seemed to Nicholas, lest haply evil befall it. Strange and subtle questions were being asked as to the origin of evil as well as to its practical mitigation. The theology of the schoolmen was being dissected, and the great Thomas of Aquin himself made to appear on the side of the new thinkers. And it was from this world, teeming with intellectual problems and hard sayings whose challenge came from the hideous actualities of the hour, that Nicholas had been exiled into the service of Sir Simon, this excellent man whose narrow outlook had already displayed itself sufficiently to reduce his new curate's spirits to a point below zero.

His cogitations were interrupted by his companion. Sir Simon pointed with his thumb towards the chancel of the chapel. There was a building abutting on it—a somewhat unwieldy addition, from the architect's point of view.

"That's an anchorhold," Sir Simon observed. "Thou wilt have to see to the housling of the anchoress. She hath her own confessor from the convent yonder but she gets her housling at the right times and seasons from the chaplain through the little window that I will show thee within." Young Nicholas the chaplain received the information with an access of depression. He surveyed the anchorage with its restricted dimensions enclosing a living soul. To him it typified the whole miserable thing; the turn his own life had taken—and after months of fervent prayer—first the backwater and now the anchorhold!

"I don't know much about her," Sir Simon continued. "They say she's uncommon holy. She's walled up and can't go abroad. Grammercy," he added. He evidently regarded it as a desirable precaution in the case of uncommon holy ladies. Nicholas might have smiled at another time. "Folks stop on their journey along the highway there—it's quite near—to have a word with her—those that have time to waste," he went on. "Quite a lot of curious folks that like to amuse themselves with something out of the common."

Had the new chaplain possessed a more intimate knowledge of Sir Simon's psychology he might have drawn the inference that the anchoress's visitors were persons whom the good rector would have been quite pleased to entertain himself had they found it worth while to diverge from their way in the direction of the Rectory. As it was he pursued the upward path in a state of deepening dejection. The path branched off in the direction of the anchorage, leading the visitor to the narrow parlour window. It was guarded by a low hedge which, with the church wall, made a little private alley of approach. There were sweet flowers growing on either side in carefully tended beds, lending an air of cheerfulness to the scene.

Sir Simon hurried on quickly past the diverging path. He was evidently afraid that his new curate might fall under the spell which drew the visitors from the high road. He produced a big key and made haste to introduce the chantry chaplain to his domain.

Nicholas knelt on the altar step and prayed for courage and resignation to support existence under the cramped conditions which should imprison his soul. It was with an aching dissatisfaction in his heart that he looked round the little chapel. He pictured its congregation of fisher-folk with their intellectual and spiritual limitations as he knelt there before One who had made of such material fishers of men. Did the latter thought come into the mind of the young man from Oxford?

Sir Simon tapped him on the shoulder. "Yonder's the anchoress's squint," he whispered pointing to a slit in the chancel wall. "'Tis through there that thou giv'st her housling. She watcheth the altar through there and heareth Mass. She may be there now," he added, dropping his voice cautiously.

It gave Nicholas a queer, eerie feeling. This anchoress was a presiding spirit—an embodiment of the spirit of the place which she haunted. She was a survival of things that were surely bound to give place to a new order. He was "modern" enough to feel repelled by the ideal that she represented. What illusions might one not go on hugging in such a fastness, looking through a slit in the wall into a building a little larger than one's own dwelling; or out of the other window at one tiny corner of the earth. He rose to his feet and followed Sir Simon to the end of the church to be instructed in the use of the big door-key, which possessed eccentricities that needed explaining. The rector inserted it in the lock of the open door and turned it for informative purposes. It made a loud, grating sound. This was almost immediately followed by another sound—that of someone singing—a muffled sound, but distinctly local. It came from the direction of the sanctuary—a sacred song sung in soft, sweet tones of bird-like richness of quality. The full, round, warbling note that no skill in teaching has ever yet been able to produce from the human throat, but which is a natural gift of great rarity. Even Sir Simon was spell-bound. "It's the anchoress," he whispered. "Listen! She heard the key turn and thought we had gone."

They stood there and listened. When it ceased they let themselves out quietly.

"If only I could get that for my miracle play," the parson muttered. "What a voice! To think of a voice like that walled up in a cell and never a soul to enjoy it. Why canst not the woman come out and be useful?"

"It sounded wonderfully distinct," Nicholas said. "Exactly as though it were in the church itself." He could not get over the idea that it might have been something supernatural.

"Oh, that was because she would be kneeling close up to the little window," Sir Simon explained, "looking at the pyx. Singing is one of her ways of saying her prayers, I've been told. 'Ods bodikins! What waste! To think that she might be singing to my guildsmen on Corpus Christi an' but for this shutting herself up in a cell."

For the first time it seemed that Sir Simon and his new curate were viewing things from the same standpoint. Yet as Nicholas turned the matter over in his mind he found himself still at variance with the ideals of the shepherd of the outlying sheepfold. Honest Sir Simon's limitations had taken their place cheek by jowl with his own aspirations. It was a confusing state of things to be thought over and combed out at his leisure.

Nicholas the Chaplain

As is very often the case that leisure did not arrive until Nicholas was in bed, and then he very sensibly employed it in dropping off to sleep. Whether his dreams succeeded in throwing light on the problem I leave it to the reader to judge, but at any rate Nicholas dreamt that he was standing in the chapel yard, amongst the graves on the cliff-side, gazing out to sea. There was a tall Calvary erected there, near the edge of the cliff, Sir Simon had displayed it to him with some pride, and now it found its way into his dream. Nicholas dreamt that he was standing close to the foot of this Calvary as he gazed seaward. His thoughts had turned towards the distant cities that he longed to visit. (The musty scent of a library rather than the sea-salt entered into his dream, for Nicholas was homesick for the stuffy odour of ancient leather bindings.) Ancient seats of learning, like Mechlin and the Rhine cities lay yonder. Then in his dreams Nicholas became conscious that someone was standing near regarding him with curiosity, and here the typical dream fantasy commenced. It was a figure such as he had become familiar with at Oxford. That of a distinguished-looking man dressed in the travelling garb of a monastic dignitary. The newcomer was evidently amused at the startled way in which Nicholas became aware of his presence. He smiled and told him that he had seen him from the distance and taken him for a statue—a St. John added to the rood. Nicholas answered smartly, as one often does in a dream. "Verily a statue erected to idleness, for I was but dreaming—there is nought else to do in this place." Then the other had answered (it was a queer dream). "Nay, that existeth already—see, up yonder. Thou art not more idle than He!" "Nay," Nicholas had answered, "but He is suffering." "And so art thou," the other had replied, "for none can approach so near to the Cross without suffering; but it is well worth it, for it is only by standing at the foot of the Cross that one can view the world from God's point of view. We get His outlook if we go up close enough, and stand quite still."

In his dream Nicholas gave vent to his inward distemper. "I am not redeeming the world," was his retort. "God seemeth far away."

"Perhaps thou art standing so near to the Cross that thou canst not see the Christ with thy bodily eyes—as it was with Our Blessed Lady," the other suggested—it was an extraordinarily vivid dream—"she could only feel the cross quivering in its socket."

"Who art thou?" Nicholas had asked, and then the dream became fantastic again. "I am the Abbot of Westminster, and I am on my way to call upon the anchoress yonder," the stranger replied, "I have grave matters on hand and would fain have her counsel." (Nicholas laughed over this part of the dream when he woke up.) "Is the anchoress so learned, or a saint?" he asked. "Neither," the dream-stranger replied, "but, thou seest, she standeth so very near to the Cross, and she standeth so very still, that she seeth things from God's point of view, and that helpeth me mightily."

At this point Nicholas had woken up. He carried the dream in his mind whilst he walked over to say his Mass, and he recounted certain parts of it to Sir Simon afterwards at breakfast. The idea of the Lord Abbot of Westminster visiting the anchoress would certainly tickle His Reverence.

His Reverence, however, seemed to miss the humour of the thing. "Who hast told thee that the Abbot of Westminster visited the anchoress on his way north?" he enquired. "I say it was all nonsense made up by the nuns."

He turned the subject, and Nicholas was left with new food for thought. Dreams were queer things: He must have absorbed the nun's canard through the pores of his understanding for he had no recollection of having been told anything of the kind.

That afternoon he went over to introduce himself to his flock, and as he climbed the cliff it occurred to him to examine the Calvary to see how far it coincided with the one in his dream. In the latter the eyes of the Christ had been gazing out seaward, like his own. He approached the Cross and looked up. The dream failed to hold good for the head of the dying Saviour was drooping, and the eyes were cast down—fixed upon the sea-shore where the little band of fishermen—Nicholas's flock—were engaged in mending their nets.

But it was not until later that Nicholas the chaplain realised that, like Pilate's wife, he had suffered things in a dream, and that the things which we suffer in a dream are likewise to be found in our waking moments by those who have eyes to see.

Chapter IX

The Parlour Window

NICHOLAS THE CHAPLAIN sat on the seat outside the anchoress's parlour window. He leant forward with his elbows on his knees and his chin resting on his interlocked fingers, and gazed hard at nothing in particular, unless it was the broad cross of white linen let into the black curtain which covered the window in accordance with the rule laid down for anchorholds. He was listening to the voice on the other side of the curtain commenting upon his own outpouring. Nicholas had occupied the window-seat for about half-an-hour, and the last twenty-five minutes had been filled with an engrossing delineation of the interior part of that intensely interesting personage, Nicholas the chaplain—the part which escaped the observation of Sir Simon the parson and his lordship the bishop. He had postponed his visit to the anchoress as long as he decently could, and had intended to make it as brief as possible—the anchorhold exemplified the moribund spirit of a dying era, he could have little in common with its inmate, holy though she might be—but here he was, taking no count of the passing of time, pouring out the story of his spiritual pains and perplexities—of his thwarted aspirations. The unseen listener had drawn him out in some marvellous way until he found himself confiding to her the innermost sorrows of his trammelled spirit. The process had been so natural. The woman behind the curtain was so absolutely the courteous lady, having some learning and much culture, the type he had come across at Oxford in the great houses, that there had been no constraint. Nicholas the chaplain had let himself go, encouraged by a sense of being listened to and understood, albeit that the comments had been few and the interruptions infrequent; and being understood was balm in Gilead for the soul of the Oxford exile. Now he had come to a pause in his recital. He had told the occupant of the cell of the great crying world and its problems—of the great struggle going on in the mid-stream. Men were asking to be made to understand the dark sayings of life, and none attempted the answers save those who were the enemies of Holy Church. Oh, for the power to press back the walls within which the souls of those in authority suffered themselves to dwell, for the key to the problem—the great overweening problem of evil—must be in possession of the Guardian of the Truth.

It was daring language, and the simile was not perhaps the happiest that could have been employed in speaking to a lady dwelling incluse. Nicholas pulled up his outpouring and waited for an answer.

"Yet it is also necessary that we dwell between four walls," the occupant of the anchorhold answered, "in order that we may first learn Truth. We must see Truth in isolation from that which dilutes or contaminates it. Truth is God alonely, untouched by that which is us. He that would show God must know God, so he must build up four walls to keep away that which hindereth a true knowing of God. That is to say, from one side cometh self-will, which is the hindering of God's omnipotence working in us; and so that we choose our own way, which is less excellent than God's way. And against this we build up the wall of meek obedience. And from another side cometh self-indulgence and sloth, which hindereth charity which is God's working in us, and against this we build up the wall of gallant chastity. And from a third side cometh self-reliance which maketh man to depend upon his own strength, nor think to seek God in prayer; and against this is built up the wall of humble prayerful dependence and reverent fear. And from the fourth side there cometh the selfness which is mistrustfulness of God, whereby we end at self and so despair and are overcome by our frailty; and against this we build the wall of trust and hopeful courage which keepeth away despondency and doleful doubts. And in the centre of these shall dwell Truth such as is God in His essence, and one dwelling there with Him shall gain true knowing of Him, or so it seemeth to me," she added, "since that I came here. When thou hast God thus thou shalt have a true seeing of Him. 'Tis self that maketh our image of what appeareth to be Him. When we hold the image of Him as He is then all is made clear and sweet and medeful."

"Then thou holdest," Nicholas said, "that a knowledge of God is of itself enough for the healing of all the sores that are festering in the body of the nations?"

"Yea," she answered, "he who hath full knowledge of God hath full understanding of all things. He alone seeth the whole world who seeth God, and as it were, seeth Him in a point; and seeing Him so, seeth that He is all good. Thou must learn to see God simple and united if thou wilt see Him in Truth."

"Then thou thinkest that I still need to seek Him myself?" Nicholas said. It was a sufficiently new idea—new enough to be striking.

"Yea," the anchoress answered simply, "but not running hither and thither. Thou canst build up thy walls here as well as anywhere else, yea, methinks better. Thou hast already built up thy wall against self-will, and choice, and thou hast the stout wall of gallant chastity against the flesh; there remaineth for thee to keep firm the wall of prayerfulness, and, or I mistake me, thou mightest begin to build up the fourth wall against doleful despondency." A smile came into the voice behind the curtain. Nicholas caught the inflection, through the white linen cross, mayhap. He smiled, and recognised that the anchoress had gently rapped his knuckles and that he deserved it. He thought for a last word.

"But thou wouldst surely have me apply myself to study?" he said. "I have that in my mind which would make a book."

"I would have thee listen," the firm voice said. "'Tis to the soul that listens that God speaketh. 'Tis a great preoccupation listening in the silence, for there must be silence in order to hear."

"But where shall I find silence?" Nicholas cried. "Amongst the screaming trivialities of this life that I have been thrust into? Sir Simon would, methinks, talk the hind leg off an ass."

There was a delightful ripple of laughter, then the voice answered gravely. "Thou must make thine own silence. Therein will lie thy preoccupation, for if I mistake not, the first man, Nicholas, who is of the earth, is as great a chatterer as His Reverence, and his thoughts will mightily interrupt the silence of the second man Nicholas, who is of heaven heavenly. It is no light task for a solitary that he be told to pray ever, 'speak, Lord, for Thy servant listeneth,' for no solitary is in sooth solitary"—Then Nicholas noted for the first time that the clear, bell-like voice of the recluse had a tired note in it as though its owner were fatigued with much travail.

He noted, too, that there was a red bar across the western sky. "Why, it groweth late," he exclaimed, "and I have worn thee out with my complaining."

"Nay," she answered, "thou hast given me much joy. Let thy complaining be but rightly set, and then be faithful to thy discontent. But remember, thou must *listen*. And let not Nicholas interrupt," she added, archly, "lest thou be not able to hear for the clatter."

Then she begged his blessing very humbly. "Thou wilt pray for the poor recluse, good father," she said softly, "for she hath been listening these three years. Pray that she listen on until He speaketh."

He caught the little sigh; and beyond the white cross he seemed to gain a sudden vision of the brave heart within, struggling in the mystical current of the mid-stream of the hidden life. She had grown a little weary building up the fourth wall of her anchorhold.

Nicholas arrived home late for the evening meal. Sir Simon was an indulgent soul and he forgave the lapse, having got well along with his own repast. "I'll warrant," quoth he, with a chuckle, "that thou hast not been all this time with the anchoress."

"She's a very wonderful woman," his curate answered, evading the question with some skill.

"Hath she been singing to thee?" Sir Simon asked.

"I forgot all about the singing," Nicholas said.

"Why, didst thou not tell her that we caught her at it?" the other cried. "But perhaps that was thy cunning. Thou canst play the same trick with the key another time."

He enjoyed his own joke boisterously, and evidently expected the other to appreciate it equally. It was an innocent jest enough but young Sir Nicholas felt no particular moving to mirth. He thought of the anchoress's words "thou must make thine own silence," and then as he thought of them he got understanding and realised that this silence was not that of a sour and scornful decorum but silence from the voice of pride and uncharity, for he was a marvellously apt pupil; and so he laughed with all the merry cheer that God had made native to him; and after that they launched forth into a dissertation on venison and the right dressing of pickled fish, and such dishes, and Sir Simon looked kindlier on his new curate than he had done before. And as he retired to his own chamber, a couple of hours later, Nicholas murmured softly, "Speak Lord, for Thy servant listeneth."

Chapter X

The Brown Pitcher

ODIVA STOOD erect in the centre of a shattered universe and absorbed the situation. The brown pitcher lay in fragments on the cottage floor in the midst of a brown pool of home-brewed beer. From Godiva's point of view it was a cataclysm. The brown pitcher and its contents existed no more!

At the end of the day Godiva's mother and the other children would return from their expedition to the village where her grandparents dwelt, and the brown pitcher and the home-brewed ale, a dole from the benevolent barrel of Master James the miller, who bestowed occasional largess on Godiva's widowed mother, would not be there to greet them. Corporal punishment would of course ensue (those were the days when a whisking with a good rod rested under religious approbation) and there was the humiliation of knowing that the catastrophe was exactly what would have been expected from Godiva, with her foolish dream-ridden head and lack of sense. But over and above these considerations there loomed the tragedy itself—the tragedy that appealed to Godiva's over-developed imagination—the loss of the jug with its blue band, with funny faces painted thereon, running all round, and of the home-brewed ale. What is so thrilling a representation of the irrevocable as spilt ale? To argue that it was but a common stone jug that produced the cataclysm would be to confound the incidental with the essential.

Sir Nicholas the chantry chaplain, who chanced (did I say chanced?) to be passing the open cottage door a moment later, grasped this fact with singular understanding. He paused and surveyed Godiva, white and tearless, and the scattered fragments, and the brown stream—the whole poignant study in the irrevocable—and took in the case in all its bearings. He was no Levite, albeit that he was a priest, to pass by such a spectacle on the other side.

Sir Nicholas came nearer and thrust his head inside the doorway and sought to offer Godiva ghostly consolation—ghostly because of its divine parentage. What he said was of course something in the English of Chaucer, the modern equivalent of which might be set down as "rotten luck."

His sympathy let loose the floodgates of Godiva's tears. She wept, and stemmed the torrent with her knuckles. For a ten-year-old it was a restrained outburst, all said and done. Sir Nicholas was at a loss how to mend matters. The jug, Godiva told him, was a beauty, with faces all round, and moreover the only one that they possessed. The rest of the tragedy she could not explain. How she was to have had this day all to herself, and being alone to dream dreams instead of playing stupid games with other children. How eagerly she had accepted the charge of being left behind to look after things and fetch the ale from kind Master James, and all the day to herself to dream her favourite dream—and then this had happened!

It was certainly a serious outlook. It seemed brutal to leave the small delinquent alone with her trouble, but the young priest had important business on hand. Like Godiva he was enjoying the unusual treat of a day to himself. Sir Simon the rector had ridden off to Northstowe to call on the bishop anent the subversion of a holy bequest for a dozen waxen candles for the altar of St. Catherine, since demolished, to the bodily needs of the poor, and Nicholas had seized the occasion to make his way to the cliff-side to visit the anchoress. Sir Simon showed no cordiality in the matter of the visits that his curate paid to the anchorhold built up against his chapel.

The anchoress had no small number of visitors from a distance. They rode along the swerving high road, giving the parish church and rectory the cold shoulder in a most invidious manner, and dismounted at the foot of the ascent leading to the chapel-of-ease. Some of these were people whom Sir Simon would have been delighted to entertain himself. He disapproved of the morbid curiosity that took them instead to the parlour window of the walled-in woman in the anchorhold, and consequently he discouraged his curate from indulging in a similar vagary. He had found little or nothing himself to say to the anchoress on the few occasions when he had visited her, and he failed to make out why his curate should seek recourse thither. Dame Catherine possessed her own confessor at the convent.

Sir Nicholas looked at the weeping child and hesitated, and then he came out with the amazing suggestion that caused another revolution in Godiva's universe.

"Wouldst thou like to come along with me and see the holy mother anchoress?" he enquired.

It is certain that had Godiva been holding a second jug of brown ale at that moment that it would have shared the fate of the first. She looked up at Sir Nicholas and gasped. The holy mother anchoress was the personality that gave all its colour to Godiva's world. If she walked for a mile and stood in a certain position on the high road she could catch an actual glimpse of the cell in which the holy lady lived immured. Saints in heaven, queens at court, fairies in their hill fastnesses—not one of these so effectually personified a figure of romance to Godiva as did the holy mother anchoress. It had never so much as occurred to her that the holy mother could be accessible to the likes of herself. It certainly had never occurred to anyone to offer to take Godiva to the enchanted spot. As far as accessibility was concerned it might have been in heaven, like the thrones of the saints, or built up, like St. Celestino's cell in the midst of the halls of the Vatican. Godiva drew ceaseless and unfailing delight from her distant contemplation of the anchorhold, and from hearing occasional allusions made to visits paid to the holy lady immured therein. She craved with a passionate but unsuspected longing to go to Mass at the fisher folks' church, but the strength of her desire would never have suggested to the timid little dreamer to play truant, and visit on her own account the chapel containing the little window through which the anchoress received her housling. Such a departure from the normal was unthought of, for like many dreamers and mystics of a larger growth Godiva was the bond-slave of the normal. She stopped crying and stood gazing at Sir Nicholas with wonder-stricken eyes.

"Oh!" she gasped at last. And then she added, "but will she let me? Will she let me see her?"

"Of course she won't," Sir Nicholas said, "Nobody ever does." Then he made haste to explain, for Godiva had mistaken his assumed gravity. "No one ever sees the anchoress. She sits behind her curtain and talks without being seen." Godiva had no need to be told this. Did not half the fascination of the fairy tale of the anchorhold lie in the fact that none had ever seen the anchoress except her serving-women, who were nuns living in the convent, another fairy castle in Godiva's wonderland. No, not since the day when they had enclosed her long ago. And they said that she was as beautiful as an angel. "But come along," Sir Nicholas added. "Perhaps thou wilt see Pusskin, the holy mother's cat, who never eats birds, and the flowers that her friends have planted along the path leading to her window."

Godiva drew in a long breath. Her whole being throbbed. She had forgotten the broken pitcher and the spilt ale. She stepped forward, right into the dreary pool of the latter, and slipped her hand into Sir Nicholas's proffered one. He had certainly chanced upon a most efficacious solace for her soul. He was thoroughly glad now that he had yielded to the impulse to saddle himself with this small companion.

The pair traversed the village street. The immensity of the occasion made Godiva a sober and silent companion. Sir Nicholas set it down to the disaster, and the sombre prospect of the evening when the parent returned. At the end of the straggling street they came upon Martha, the good dame who kept house for Sir Simon. They stopped, and Sir Nicholas told her of the tragedy in outline, and Godiva filled it in with details of the blue band and the funny faces, and shed some more tears in so doing. Martha was the kindest soul alive. "Well, well," she said, "thou must ask the good mother anchoress to pray that thy pitcher be mended." Godiva was dreadfully scandalised. The idea of the holy lady who was shut up in a cell in order that she might see nothing but holy visions being asked to give attention to such a sundry as a brown pitcher, and one with funny faces all round, to boot—such funny faces, too! When they reached the green slope leading up to the cliff Godiva's heart thumped quite painfully. There stood the chapel, high up in front of them as they entered the rough enclosure, and there was the glimpse of the anchorhold, the nearest that Godiva had ever obtained. Now they were actually walking up the path leading to it. Sir Nicholas had first paused and examined the trunk of the large yew tree at the foot of the ascent, explaining to her that when the anchoress was in stricter seclusion than usual her attendants fastened a white cross to the tree to warn visitors off. Godiva felt convinced that had the cross been there at the present moment she would have died on the spot from disappointment. It would in sooth have been worse than the pitcher.

As they climbed the path her companion pointed out other features of interest, the little apertures under the eaves of the reed thatch that gave light to the cell apart from its curtained window. He also told her about the other little window through which the enclosed lady watched him say his Mass and received Our Lord in Holy Communion. Godiva listened enthralled. She had heard it all before but now she was actually on the spot. I won't attempt to deny that fairyland was even more present in her mind than heaven. Still, the great, outstanding thrill came from the sense of the awesome holiness of the recluse lady who had given up a big, big castle, and lovers and jewels, to embark on this strange adventure. Somehow to Godiva it seemed explicable. Big castles and fine clothes could not produce the thrill in her soul that this strange anchorhold could. But it would not have been thrilling save that the anchoress had been, once on a time, a rich lady and as beautiful as an angel. The price of the field containing the treasure was a distant factor in Godiva's "fairy tale."

So she unconsciously analysed the mystery of worship—of sacrifice—the charm which works on the souls of those who renounce all, and Sir Nicholas, leading her by the hand, felt the small palm grow moist within his own. He, too, was by way of being highly wrought in his soul, for he was about to consult the anchoress—to ask her prayers—on a matter of the utmost importance. Nicholas had been committing to paper, no light thing in those days, the result of his cogitations on certain problems of the hour that were making no small stir in the outside world. He was a true and loyal son of holy Mother Church, but there were some fierce denunciations of things that pertained to her ministers in Nicholas's screed. John Wyclif's "poor priests" were thundering a wild doctrine throughout the land, and its echoes tinged the thoughts of many a young idealist who took scandal at the abuses of an ill-shepherded age. The screed that had grown under his pen during the long months that he had been moored in these stagnant waters was full of the tumultuous yearnings of his heart, the glowing images, and eke the biting sarcasms, which rose in his mind as he wrote, albeit that he started his work with prayer, and sanctified it with acts of mortification and penance. He had launched his barbed missiles at the second best, the circumscribed, the effete, and the very efficiency of his work had given rise to a qualm of conscience, for in tearing out the cockle, might he not have inadvertently touched the wheat? He could pass his MS. on to a friend at Oxford who would make good use of it, but this friend was himself not untouched by the new thought. He might read into the words of Nicholas a meaning that the author never intended.

He would fain have shown the screed as it stood to the holy mother anchoress but Dame Catherine abode under a strict rule which forbade her from taking spiritual reading save that approved by her confessor, and Nicholas had no fancy for submitting his MS. to the aged and holy man up at the convent, who was, if possible, more archaic than Sir Simon. So young Sir Nicholas refrained from pouring his new and precious vintage into the ancient receptacle lest it should indeed be lost. He contented himself with communicating the gist of its contents to the anchoress on the occasions of his visits. These occasions were becoming rarer for the good parson managed to find plenty of work to keep his curate busy, and there was no time after Mass to linger at the anchorhold window. Hence it will be seen that young Sir Nicholas had wrought a work of considerable self-abnegation in saddling himself with a companion on this particular occasion.

Godiva, drinking in the stupendousness of the occasion, fully appreciated the silence which had fallen upon her companion. The path had taken a sideways turn, for they had reached the summit of the ascent and were close up to the chapel, with its sturdy grey walls and buttresses, and quaint beacon tower. A level walk, trim and well kept, led along to the anchorhold. It was bordered by a carefully clipped hedge, beneath which there flourished in profusion flowers of every description—violets, lilies of the valley, and daffodils galore, ladening the air with sweetness. Godiva was enraptured. Flowers were indeed living things to her. The anchoress's serving-maidens tended her garden, Sir Nicholas told her, and Godiva's heart thrilled at the thought of so blissful an office. When there was no one there the holy mother drew back the curtain and looked upon her garden, Nicholas told Godiva, for it might be that God walked there Himself in the evening-time; and it might be that His angels had really planted the daffies and violets, not the serving-maidens after all. They were approaching the little curtained window, and now Godiva had eyes for nothing else. Sir Nicholas gave a gentle tug at an iron chain on the hedge and a little bell tinkled ever so softly. Godiva held her breath. It was the moment of her life, for surely so exquisite a moment could be experienced by no one more than once in a lifetime?

Chapter XI

The Miracle

HEY SAT DOWN, side by side, on the stone seat and waited. There was a faint sound within. Then an unseen hand adjusted the curtain with the large white cross which was all but transparent, so that no corners were left to act as peep-holes. Then a very pleasant voice said, "*Dominus tecum*," in a slightly interrogative tone. "*Et cum spiritu tuo*," Sir Nicholas responded, in quite an "at home" tone. The inmate of the cell recognised the voice and there came the seemly response, "Thy blessing, good father." Godiva pictured the owner of the voice kneeling on the other side of the curtained window as Sir Nicholas raised his hand and gave the required blessing. Then he looked at Godiva and smiled. "I have brought thee a visitor, holy mother," he said. "It is Godiva, and she is ten years old—nearly grown up—and she hath come to thee for solace for she is in great trouble and perplexity."

Godiva blushed furiously under the description of herself and her business. She could not have grown pinker had the holy Mother's eye been verily upon her.

"What is thy trouble, Godiva?" the voice asked, in tones of kindly concern.

Godiva was speechless and confounded. Sir Nicholas, of his charity, explained for her. "It's the brown pitcher," he said. "Godiva was left in charge of the cottage and the brown pitcher let itself fall and got smashed, and it's the only one."

"Oh, dear!" the voice said, "Poor little Godiva!"

Poor little Godiva got three shades pinker with confusion. But worse was to come. "It had funny faces all round it," Sir Nicholas went on, solemnly, "and it was full of home-brewed ale."

"But can't it be mended?" the holy lady enquired in tones verging on anxiety, whilst Godiva listened and gaped.

"It's in fifty pieces," Sir Nicholas replied.

"Well, we must pray that it comes all right," the voice said, after a silence that suggested cogitation.

Godiva sat entranced, and be it added, just a little scandalised. Here was the holy Lady of her dreams actually speaking, and she listening; and she was not speaking of ghostly things but of her brown jug. And it was such an interested voice! Godiva ached with desire to see its owner. The voice was so gentle and full of kindness. It would be such an *interested* face. She gazed at the curtain. The anchoress had indeed become shorn of some of her mystery, but there was in her place a real, living woman, whose eyes, Godiva felt, would be kind and tender, and seeing. They said she was beautiful. Godiva felt convinced that she was.

Sir Nicholas watched the child's expressive face. It interested him, but he had his own axe to grind, and he could not safely grind it with a child's wide ears open at his side.

The lady behind the curtain settled the difficulty with the tact of a hostess in the world manipulating her guests.

"Godiva has never been to see me before," she observed, "she must gather some violets to carry away with her to remember me by. The white ones grow at the end of the path. Wouldst thou like to gather some, childkin?"

So Godiva found herself gently dismissed from the enchanted spot. The end of the path was not far off, however, and whilst she gathered her violets she could gaze ever and anon at the window against which Sir Nicholas sat, leaning forward and speaking with great vivacity. He would be having ghostly conversation with the holy lady, not discoursing on pitchers and brown ale. She stopped picking violets and watched with fascinated eyes. She could just catch the murmur of his voice and watch the play of expression on his eager, boyish face. She sat there on her heels with the violets in her lap in an ecstasy of contentment, which was, however, tinged with the pain of longing, not merely longing to listen to the enchanted voice—she did not grudge kind Sir Nicholas his private conversation (the delicacy which made Godiva a dreamer, not to be trusted with the custody of a jug of brown ale, also lent her the perception to grasp that the conversation was private) but a new and overweening desire to see the hidden face behind the curtain. Godiva's falling in love was antecedent to first sight. She pictured the face, beautiful and eager, like Sir Nicholas's. He must be speaking of something very ghostly for his face was just like it looked when he preached to the people at Vespers. No, it was certainly not about brown pitchers, and—she blushed at the recollection—pitchers with funny faces all round. Godiva sat there in exquisitive happiness for perhaps an hour. Then Sir Nicholas rose and looked round for his charge. He beckoned her to him. Godiva scrambled to her feet, regardless of pins and needles and hastened back to be once more within the pale of the voice. The priest turned to the window. "Thou wilt pray, holy mother," he said, reiterating the burden of his conference. "Indeed I will," the unseen lady replied, "that this shall happen to thy work which is for the best. If thou hast written it within the anchorhold that I told thee of, there should not be anything amiss with it, but remember always the anchorhold which containeth Truth and keepeth away error."

Her listener glanced apprehensively at the child whose presence the anchoress needed to be warned of. "And thou wilt pray for Godiva," he said, "that it may be well with her and her broken pitcher?" The hint was effective.

"Why verily I will," the anchoress replied, heartily. "Godiva, I will not forget the brown jug. I will pray that thou gettest another with funny faces. Good-bye. Thou wilt come and see me again and tell me how it hath fared with thee. If thou art really and truly ten years old thou mightest find thy way hither by thyself."

So Godiva left the anchorage lifted up into the seventh heaven. She and her companion were both preoccupied with their thoughts. A common bond of sympathy made them forget each other's presence with the freedom of established friendship. Godiva was marvelling once more that the holy anchoress should not only have attended to the story of her disaster, but that she should have seemed to understand so exactly what it meant to be left in charge and told not to dream dreams, and then, when you were going to prove how very sensible and reliable you were, for the brown pitcher to go and get broken. Such a thing could never have happened to the holy lady when she was in the world, for she was a princess, or something, with lots of servants to wait on her and break things.

Sir Nicholas was also reviewing his visit to the anchoress. He had talked with her concerning his literary outpouring and as he recounted the burning phrases in which he had clothed his ideas he had become convinced that his was indeed an inspired utterance—a message for the age, a counterblast to the nefarious efforts of the disciples of John Wyclif. The anchoress had been deeply interested, but she shared his apprehensions. He had longed for the MS. which he had left lying on the table in his room, beside the big horn inkstand, so that he might read her extracts, but that the anchoress had tabooed as infringing the spirit of her rule, if not the letter. "I will pray," she had said, after deep thought. "It seemeth to me that thou hast indeed a wonderful message, yet there may be danger. Tell me, hadst thou truly made firm the walls of thy anchorhold when thou didst write these things?"

Nicholas had assured her that it was so. Had he not given up his will and resigned himself to his present circumstances? He had mortified himself and prayed and kept vigil that the Holy Spirit might be his guide in all that he set down. And he had kept to his task courageously in spite of the maddening interruptions. Were not the four walls of his anchorhold sound and secure?

"Then all will be well," the anchoress had said. "I will pray that such happens to thy script as shall be for the greater glory of God."

He was thinking of that promise now, and he unconsciously hastened his footsteps as though that something might be brought to happen on the spot. Sir Nicholas had unbounded faith in the anchoress's prayers.

At that moment Godiva gave evidence that her mind was running in the same lines. She dragged him away from the vision of his script in the hands of the scholars at Oxford, preaching a vivified truth in the forceful phrases that he had scarcely felt to be his own when he had read them over. "Please, father," the voice of the child at his side asked, "dost thou think that the holy mother will really pray about my pitcher?"

Sir Nicholas was certain that she would. The anchoress was always as good as her word. Godiva detected reproach in his tones at her doubting. It seemed hard to believe. The holy mother was not like Mrs. Martha, whose sympathy had been perfectly natural. "I expect that she's praying now," Sir Nicholas said—"for both of us."

Whatever the anchoress may have been doing, Mrs. Martha, as a matter of fact, was sympathising actively with Godiva at that very minute. She was in her kitchen cutting up the meat for the pasty, and her eye happened to rest upon an array of jugs and other vessels ranged upon a shelf.

One of the former was a brown pitcher with a blue band round the middle upon which was portrayed a series of grotesque faces. It was a common pattern, one largely favoured for receptacles of the convivial brew, and was reproduced by the hundreds with the utmost exactitude of design. It was probably identical with the one that the child had broken. At any rate it brought Godiva's misfortune back to the mind of kind Mrs. Martha. It was a sad loss for the poor child, the good soul thought, being the only one that the family possessed. She ran her eye over the superabundance of receptacles on the long shelf, and recalled Godiva's tear-stained face. She somehow felt far sorrier now for the child than she had done at the time. Then she thought of the spilt ale, the gift of the charitable miller, and then of the rectory butt with its foaming contents, and that sent her thoughts off at a tangent. Had she remembered to shut out the new puppy in the yard where the butt stood?

He was a very devil of mischief. It would never do to leave him loose in the house. Sir Nicholas was careless, like all young folks, and often left his door open. Well she would see to it later. She had not yet drawn the ale for supper. Her thoughts insisted on returning to Godiva. She had peeped in the cottage, which was just opposite to the rectory, on her way in and viewed the *débris*, thus her meditation did not lack for composition of place. Memory and understanding likewise played their orthodox part, and Mrs. Martha being an eminently practical person, it might be safely presumed that a very solid resolution followed.

Sir Nicholas parted from his companion at the gate leading to the rectory. Godiva had been walking on air but as she pushed the cottage door open she felt the hard earth under her feet once again. The *débris* would have to be cleared away before her mother's return, and afterwards the sad confession made.

She entered the living-room, and stood stock still. There was no brown pool on the brick floor, and no *débris*, but on the table there stood a brown pitcher—a brown pitcher with a wide blue band round the middle. Godiva stood agape, firmly disbelieving her eyes, for at least two minutes. Then she approached the vision cautiously and inspected it. There were funny faces on the blue band—it almost seemed to Godiva that they were funnier than ever! She peeped inside the færie vessel. It was filled to the brim with foaming golden ale.

Godiva went down on to her knees. She tried to realise that a miracle had happened—a fitting ending to the adventurous day. The calamity had passed, and all was well! Oh, yes, all was wonderfully well, for behind this joy and relief was another, yet a greater joy, a joy on an entirely different plane—the holy mother anchoress was indeed a saint. She had worked a miracle by her prayers. Oh, that was lovely indeed!

Sir Nicholas also admitted himself into his domicile. He made straight for his own apartment, rather anxiously, for he remembered that he had left the door open and his script on his table. Old Martha was unlettered and could not pry into its contents, but Sir Simon might have returned early. There was a vague apprehension in his mind as he entered his chamber. The script had become very precious indeed since he had enlarged upon its contents to the understanding listener. She was praying for it, too! He felt like a knight with his lance in full tilt, out to slay dragons, as he strode into the sanctum which had been the scene of its making.

Like Godiva, he stood stock still and stared. There was no script on the table beside the horn inkstand, but on the floor there were strewn minute particles of torn paper—strips, shreds, tatters. They lay about in all directions, as though the fiend of destruction had been enjoying the time of his life in Nicholas's study.

The latter stood stupefied with horror. The record of his living words, his ideas, his interpretations, his scathings and castigations, lay before him, irrevocably lost. It must indeed be the work of the fiend who hated reformers and the thinkers of new thoughts. It was young Sir Nicholas's world which had subsided this time—that lay in pieces at his feet. It might perhaps have reminded him of the shattered pitcher and the spilt ale had he not at that moment received a more definite reminder of the sister-tragedy. There was a sound near the doorway and looking up he saw a small figure standing there—Godiva. In her hands she held a brown pitcher.

"Father, oh father," she gasped. "Look! The holy mother has mended my pitcher. I found it on the table, and it is full of ale!"

Sir Nicholas looked from the child to the jug. There were funny faces on the blue band, and it was full of golden ale. Godiva's beaming face called upon him to rejoice with her. Sir Nicholas took the jug in his hands and examined it. It was certainly a stupefying occurrence.

At that moment there appeared another visitor on the scene. The white puppy peeped cautiously in at the door. He advanced in a deprecating manner, his tail placed neatly between his legs, and laid himself on his back at Sir Nicholas's feet with his four legs in the air. Sir Nicholas went on examining the blue band and collecting his thoughts. "It *is* good of the holy mother," Godiva said, and she added, in tones that were a little scandalised, "the funny faces are funnier than ever!"

This comment enabled Sir Nicholas to fulfill the precept of rejoicing with those who rejoice with some show of genuineness. He gave a little laugh. The white puppy cheered up. It reversed its attitude, and shaking itself, stood with cocked ears asking for a game.

Godiva remembered her manners. "Has she prayed for thee, too?" she enquired. "Has the holy mother worked a miracle for thee, Father?"

Sir Nicholas started. He gazed at the enquirer without answering. An idea had struck him. Godiva waited for the answer. The white puppy waited with drooping tail. It was quite a long time in coming.

At last Sir Nicholas's face lighted up. "I believe she has, Godiva," he said, "but I will tell thee about it another day."

"I am glad," Godiva said, and the white puppy lifted its tail and trotted off in her wake to find a rat, or failing that an article of wearing apparel.

Sir Nicholas summoned Mrs. Martha to help him clear up the mess. She was horrified, but Sir Nicholas set her mind at rest.

"'Twas but some script that I should have burned myself," he explained. "I have been saved the trouble."

"But thou hadst written it all thyself, Father," the unlettered Mrs. Martha exclaimed. "To think of that, all thyself!" She threw up her hands in desolation.

Sir Nicholas smiled. "Yea, Mrs. Martha," he replied, "I had written it—all myself. That was the trouble. Now we will put the pieces in the fire."

A week later Godiva met the chaplain. "Well," he asked her, "and didst thou tell thy mother about the miracle?"

"Yea, Father, I had to. It was so wonderful," Godiva said. "But (her face falling) she said that it might have been no miracle but some kind neighbour that had a jug like ours."

Sir Nicholas comforted her. "But would it not have been just as much a miracle to make the neighbour's heart so kind as all that?" he asked.

"God works the wonders, not the person who prayeth, and He hath His way of doing them through His creatures. Why, verily, Godiva, if God liked He could even accomplish His end through a white puppy. But, whatever hath happened, thou and I will sing unto the Lord a new song, for He hath done a wonderful thing."

Chapter XII

No-Man's Danny

IT WAS THE TWENTIETH day of Lent, or thereabouts, and Dame Catherine, the anchoress, keeping the fast in accordance with her rule, was hungry. This fact is mentioned simply to account for her psychological condition, that only being of any intrinsic importance in a lady "dwelling incluse." Dame Catherine's ghostly condition may be described as one of scruples supervening on the austerities of the season.

The anchoress was entertaining a very grave scruple. It had been there for some time past, receiving scant hospitality, but to-day the recluse was entertaining it assiduously. It had arisen in connection with the visitors who frequented the parlour-window seeking ghostly counsel. During the present holy season, when she would fain have enjoyed a stricter seclusion, the visits of these "pilgrims" had occurred with increasing frequency, and the fact that it was ghostly counsel alone that was to be given from the anchorage window in no wise deterred idle folk from intruding, as in the case of young Ralph Attyard, whose lengthy preamble had but led up to the fact that he was in need of a new surcoat to wear at the fair, and that he hoped to obtain it by means of the holy mother's prayers. There were other pilgrims of a larger spiritual growth than Ralph whose visits nevertheless were a distraction. Ecclesiastics some of them; learned clerks some; and their visits were unimpeachably restricted to matters spiritual, there were also simple folk whose troubles, though irrelevant, had a legitimate claim on human sympathy. Still the anchoress entertained her scruple as to the legitimacy of the second window—that giving on the world, where the life of a solitary was to be led in its fulness. The parlour-window had proved the downfall of many a holy recluse in times gone by—especially among those of her own sex.

Even as the anchoress sat thinking the matter out there came a ring at the bell, a typical interruption.

"Who art thou?" the enclosed lady asked. "Is it ghostly counsel that thou seekest?" It was just a trifle sharply said, for there had been no sound of anyone approaching, and the sudden clang of the bell had taken her overstrained human nature unawares.

"Good mother, if thou couldst withdraw thy curtain," the visitor replied suavely, "thou wouldst not need to ask that question. Thou art speaking with a friar-preacher."

He was garbed in a rough brown habit and cord, and as he spoke he glanced down at it and adjusted the girdle, as though the other might indeed be observing him, despite the drawn curtain.

"Forgive me, good sir," the anchoress replied, repentantly. "I saw not who it was, for my rule forbiddeth me to withdraw my curtain save only that there be a grave ghostly reason for the doing so."

"A wise rule, most holy mother," the visitor replied, with increased suavity, "for all that it enableth many to approach thee with idle speech ere thou canst gain cognisance of their ilk. In sooth, for one of thy calling methinks that it would be better that there were no window at all?"

The woman within started. It was a curious speech for one to make who himself sought converse with her, but the anchoress's ready wit did not rise to the occasion. All that rose was the scruple.

"It must prove a grievous distraction, this commerce with the world," the smooth voice went on. The other could not gainsay the remark, mindful as she was of Ralph Attyard's new surcoat for the fair.

"My rule doth admit a parlour-window," she murmured. "'Tis by having speech with others that I may pass on the comfort that cometh to my own soul. 'Tis thus that I give bread to the hungry," she added softly, for she was ever answering the scruple in her heart.

"Nay, surely," the stranger responded, "God doth not look to thee to provide bread for the hungry. If bread He needeth, cannot He command the stones that they become bread?"

The other thought a while; then she replied, "Thou wouldst have me ask God that He command the stones that they become bread rather than He use an instrument of His making, as is His wont? But, in sooth," she added, "I will ask my confessor." Her tones were troubled.

"Nay," the stranger replied, quickly, "why trouble thy confessor upon such a matter when a higher source of guidance is thine. Thy soul will come to no harm by dispensing with that which is but to safeguard ordinary souls that have no special favour from Heaven. Thy soul will come to no hurt, holy mother, for is it not written that He shall give his angels charge over thee?"

"Good sir," the anchoress replied, faintly. "Thou mayest indeed be right, but hast thou the authority to speak thus to one bound by a holy vow of obedience? 'Tis not the same as one living secular in the world. It were as tempting God Himself to tempt one who obeyeth His voice in her rule."

"Now, nay, dear mother," the visitor answered, in tones of patient persuasion, "thy holy rule doth not enjoin the parlour-window, it but permits it. Without its distraction one with thy gift of prayer could work miracles and so gain the whole world to God. If thou wilt but take my advice and trouble not thy confessor with that which lieth without his jurisdiction, I promise thee that thou shalt indeed work miracles to edify the world and bring men to the Truth."

"But, good sir, my confessor is also a holy man," the anchoress retorted, warmly. "Him I obey, as it were God, Whom we all obey in that it is Him and Him alone that we must adore. But I will pray the Holy Spirit that He guide me, good sir. I would that thou prayest with me also," she added, for the scruple was still eating at her heart, and her fighting power was all but exhausted, for as has been said, the anchoress had been twenty days in the wilderness and she was hungry.

So she prayed for a space, and when at the end of the time she addressed her visitor there was no answer. She waited, and then spoke again but there was still no answer. Her visitor had quietly slipped away. But there was another approaching. She heard the footstep with a little groan for her strength was spent. Then she gave a little sound of relief for she recognised the slow footfall of her confessor, the convent chaplain, who was getting on in years and slightly lame. He sometimes visited her at the parlour-window although he possessed access to the outer cell.

"Father," she asked, "Sawest thou one just now as thou camest up the path?"

"Yea," he replied, "one wearing the habit of religion, but if I mistake not a mock friar, one of those that the heretics have sent out to do the devil's work. I liked not his gait, nor the look on his face. I noted not which way he went, he seemed to go quickly, but doubtless thou hadst given him a short shrift, dear daughter."

She was silent. "Holy father," she burst out, at last. "I have a grave matter wherein I would seek thy directing. It is concerning these visitors who come ever and anon to my window. I have come to have doubts whether it be well for me to have all this commerce with the outside world. Whether it would not be better that I sought a more strict seclusion from my kind and betook myself to prayer with God alonely."

The old man was silent, weighing the question in his mind. It was no easy one to answer. He knew well the whole bearings of the case. How this idle gossip at the parlour-window was the besetting danger of the anchorhold. He knew, moreover, that spiritual pride is a still greater danger, and the anchoress's visitors included many persons of intellectual and spiritual distinction as well as the village busybodies, whose pilgrimages might be a source of even greater danger than those of the latter. And, again, a third danger existed—that of visits from such as this mock friar who might easily insinuate the baleful heresies of the day into an impressionable mind like that of his holy penitent. There were certainly three excellent reasons for approving the anchoress's suggestion. And yet he hesitated. He was no tyro in the spiritual life not to know that contemplation requires a complete withdrawal from created images and creatures. Why he hesitated he scarcely knew. He partook himself to prayer for light. "My child," he said at last, "I would not dare to settle this matter for thee with undue haste. God may will this more privy life for thee now, or it may be later on. Pray for nine days to the Holy Spirit, and if at the end of that time thou hast no direct showing telling thee to the contrary, I will give thee permission to withdraw thyself from those who have this effect of keeping thy soul from its true vocation. But not until thou hast prayed and watched for nine days would I have thee act in so grave a matter. Meanwhile set the white cross on the tree that none may disturb thee and retire into thyself, and may the Lord give thee light."

So it fell out that the warning white cross appeared on the trunk of the yew tree and the anchoress partook herself to uninterrupted prayer, kneeling at the little inner window that looked upon the sanctuary. The undesirable visitors kept away, respecting the message designed for the benefit of the unlettered, which Felicity fixed in its place assisted by Perpetua. "'Twill be but for a day or two," the latter commented with her usual pessimism, "and it keepeth not off the stranger, only the folk from round about that could make one cry for the dulness of their tales."

"I would rather that the stranger were kept off than they," Felicity answered, "'Tis homely for the dear mother to have these about her that are friends and can tell her of those that she loveth." Felicity and Perpetua continued to survey life from different aspects.

It is doubtful, though, whether even Felicity would have approved of the visitor who in spite of the warning approached the anchoress's cell on the night of the ninth day of the novena. It was the Saturday of Passion week. A pitch dark night with a sea-mist enveloping the land on the border of the cliff, and it happened that "No-man's Danny," the most negligible piece of humanity in the neighbourhood, found himself stranded in the vicinity of the beacon chapel. The beacon was not burning—it was seldom lighted now-a-days—but Danny could just discern the outline of the church. He had tumbled up against the rough wall encircling the graveyard and climbed over, for he durst not move in the direction of the cliff lest he should fall over and reach home precipitately. The cove hamlet represented home to No-man's Danny, in a sort of generalized way. He was a waif and stray, the bastard off-spring of one of the fisher lasses who had abandoned him there and gone back to the abyss of the world she had chosen. Danny had grown up promiscuously, subsisting on the chance benevolence of the community, like a little stray animal. A queer, weird, wild creature he had grown into consequently, and for the same reason was set down by the cottars as one of God's fools, although the Good God had in no wise constructed his intellect differently from others. Running wild and eating and sleeping where he could was the normal existence of No-man's Danny. It presented no conscious problem to his inarticulate mind. Loneliness and isolation were sometimes a definite sense in his heart. Tonight, for example, No-man's Danny had a distinct feeling of being a self-contained unit in the social economy of the world he lived in. He was horribly lonely and more than a little afraid. He gravitated towards the chapel because he had picked up some religion in his precarious education, thanks to the fact that he lived in the dark ages, and it represented protection against the perils of the night. But, on the other hand, the presence of the dead men under the mounds over which he was stumbling was a fearsome thing that chilled the marrow in his bones. The touch of the grue increased the misery of his situation, but No-man's Danny was a philosophical soul, and being out at night was no new experience to him, for he habitually slept out of doors in the summer. He took a survey of the situation and remembered that there was, after all, another living being near at hand—one who had no objection to dwelling near the dead. Just beside the anchoress's window, moreover, in a particularly snug corner, there was a long seat which would offer quite a comfortable bed—high and dry, and sheltered. Danny had not the faintest intention of disturbing the inmate of the cell, whom he would never have dreamt of approaching, even at authorised hours. He had never done more than peep along the flower-lined path after he had crept away from Mass on Sundays. But there was no occasion to intrude on the anchoress. No-man's Danny was as noiseless in his movements as a rabbit or any other small mammal. He found his way to the anchorage path and crept softly up to the seat under the window. It was beautifully protected from the sea-damp, and there was a sense of protection about the whole place that was welcome to the heart of the waif and stray suffering from the pain of loneliness and dereliction. He stretched his body out on the bench and prepared to sleep, for he was tired and exhausted, though not overpoweringly hungry, thanks to the alms of a vagabond on the road. Rogues and vagabonds figured largely amongst No-man's Danny's benefactors. The Good God probably thrust him in their way that they might have the honour of doing it to the least of the little ones. In a very few minutes sleep had overtaken him and he was slumbering every whit as peacefully as the king's son in his bed of feathers.

Chapter XIII

The Showing

ITHIN THE ANCHORAGE sleep had also claimed Dame Catherine. She was permitting herself a night of comparative rest in prudent preparation for the watches of the Passion, when she would take on her willing shoulders, for love of Him who suffered in Gethsemane, the task allotted to Peter, James and John, of which they had acquitted themselves so poorly. Tonight she would wake for one hour and then retire to rest. Her nine days of prayer had so far brought no direct showing from Heaven to deter her from following the course that she had submitted to her spiritual guide. The closing of the outer window seemed to be the way of perfection—the only road to union with God, in Himself alonely—"the jealous Lover who suffereth no fellowship." She thought of Sir Nicholas the chaplain with his eager struggles—how he would hear of the decision with dismay. Of Godiva, with her awakening soul and shy confidences; of many others who left her little window and went on their way to slay dragons, as though invigorated with a draught of wine; and of the simple souls who loved the sound of her voice and the scent of her flowers. She thought of all these things until she fell asleep, like No-man's Danny.

She had been sleeping deeply and dreamlessly when she awoke with a sudden start, and a feeling that she had slept too long. It would be time for her hour's vigil. It was pitch dark, and in the suddenness of her waking she sprang from her bed and found herself standing in the centre of her cell before she was thoroughly awake. She groped her way to the little inner window and felt for her kneeling-stool. It was not there, so she threw herself on her knees on the hard ground (as He had done) and peered out into the darkness. But it should not have been darkness. They had forgotten to replenish the sanctuary lamp. It was not burning in its accustomed place! The most holy Sacrament had been left in the dark. It emphasised the aloneness of the Dweller on the altar, in the little hanging pyx. There was no light to symbolise the Presence, and the unforgottenness of that Presence, for all its solitude.

To the ordinary devout worshipper such a discovery would have brought a sense of unseemliness—of irreverence, it might be of sacrilege. To the recluse, it meant all these things, but over and above all, swamping these considerations, there came a sudden piercing of the heart, a feeling of compunction. A true daughter of her age, in her the personal Christ had not been alienated from the human passions of the soul of man. Dame Catherine saw out in the darkness the slighted Lover, the forgotten and unaccompanied Friend of humanity suffering a mystical continuance of His agony in the garden. A pang of compassion wrung her heart, and gave vent to itself in a burst of words.

"My dear! My dear! My sweeting! They have left Thee all alone!

"What have they done to Thee?" she went on. "They have forgotten Thee. Nay, here will I stay till dawn and my heart shall be Thy lamp."

So she bent her head and stayed there, thinking on His loneliness and His longing, and of the mean response of the ever-divided human heart. Was there in the wide world one that was His alone—one anchorhold that possessed but one window? She knelt there expressing the thoughts that were in her heart in the manner that came natural to her. She had become a sanctuary lamp. "My dear, my sweeting," she repeated, "Thou art not alone, for I am watching with Thee. Thou art mine own for dost Thou not belong to me?" It was the tender language of the devotion of the age—that feature of mediæval mysticism that the later ages can only gaze upon over the chasm of desecrating years, wondering at its exceeding simplicity, and the sweet mother-note it contained.

Outside the anchorage No-man's Danny turned in his sleep. He opened his eyes. Like the enclosed lady he had discovered that strange things can happen to those who seek their rest up against the walls of a sanctuary. Then he turned over and closed them again, for it was still dark.

But in spite of her willing spirit the anchoress's flesh was but the flesh of Peter, James and John. Ere the first streak of dawn had come to relieve her of her watch her head had fallen forward and she was fast asleep, overcome by the weariness of her overtaxed body. She dreamt that she was assisting at Mass, and in her dream she heard the sacring bell ring. She woke up with a start. Surely enough a bell was ringing, the little bell against her window. She gazed out in front of her. The dim daylight was peering in upon her through a white cross let into a black curtain. She was kneeling in front of her parlour-window!

She had no time to collect her thoughts for a voice was already addressing her from outside. It was that of a young fisher lad. He had come in search of her prayers, ignoring or else omitting to notice, the forbidding sign on the tree. His father lay in his death agony and he had hastened to catch the priest on his way to say Mass that he might implore him to come without delay and shrive the dying man and give him housling. He had come round to the anchoress's window to beg her good prayers that the priest might arrive in time.

"Yea, verily I will pray," the anchoress answered, and there shot through her mind the thought that this would be the last time that such a one, with such a request, would ring her bell. "But," she added, for her mind, like that of more mystics than the world imagines, was prompt and practical in its dealings with the concrete, "hadst thou not better get on thy way or thou wilt miss the priest, he may be even now approaching."

"Nay, that will be all right," the lad answered, "for I met the child that they call No-man's Danny coming away from here and I bade him watch for Sir Nicholas and stay him on his way till I returned if haply he came along. The lad hath a queer head but he is good enough for that!"

"What was he doing here?" the anchoress enquired. "'Tis a strange name for a child, 'No-man's Danny'?"

"He told me he had slept under thy window," the lad replied. "He answereth to the name well enough, but," he went on, "he was queer just now when I called it out to him. 'Hi!' quoth I, 'come here, No-man's Danny,' and he looked at me, all smiling, and with a gay cheer and he sayeth; 'I be not No-man's Danny, I be God's Danny. He hath told me so Hissel'.'"

He had lingered in spite of his haste as though he felt impelled to relate the strange retort of the simpleton. The child's face had been so full of joy. It haunted him. He moved off quickly now and left the anchoress to sort out the situation in her mind. She rose and dragged her stiffened limbs over to the other little window. Through it she saw the sanctuary lamp burning faithfully before the altar. Yea, without doubt she had been kneeling all through the night in the place where she had just found herself. She had failed to see the sanctuary light, not because it wasn't there but because she had been kneeling at the other window—the parlour-window looking out on to the world.

As she grasped the truth a sense of keen disappointment seized upon her. So after all she had not been allowed to keep Him company—to console Him in His loneliness. Her words of love had been wasted—they had gone out of the other window, and fallen on the ears of none—yea, of one—of a waif and stray who was known as "No-man's Danny." Yea, but who was now "God's

Danny." "I be not No-man's Danny. I be God's Danny. I heerd Him tell me so Himself."

"Thou art not alone. I am watching with thee for thou art mine, my dear, my sweeting." Those were the words that had fallen on the ears of No-man's Danny.

The anchoress knelt at the little inner window a-thinking. The moments passed but she knelt on with bowed head. Mother Catherine was receiving her showing—at the end of her nine days' prayer. There had been no miscarriage of her loving intent. Her voice had not been misdirected. In the dark hours of the night she had indeed consoled Him in His loneliness in the person of one of these little ones.

Once again a bell sounded. This time it was verily the sacring bell. She looked up and saw Sir Nicholas the chaplain through her little window. He was coming away from the altar bearing something in his hands. Beside him there walked a ragged urchin carrying a lighted lantern in one hand and a bell in the other. No-man's—no, God's Danny, had evidently caught the priest and delivered the message, and apparently he was acting as acolyte. Sir Nicholas the chaplain was taking the holy viaticum to the dying fisherman. He had taken it from the pyx over the altar, but the sanctuary lamp still burned for the pyx still retained the mystic treasure, its sum undiminished. He who was wending His way far afield was still present on the altar. His going forth need in no wise turn the worship of His lover from the sacred place where He rested in His Holy Mystery. All this Dame Catherine learned in the ghostly showing that was hers as she knelt there listening, with her ears very meekly opened, for, it seemed to her that the going out and the abiding were but two windows looking upon the same thing.

Later in the day she received a visit from her confessor.

"Daughter," the old man said, "hath God revealed to thee His will concerning thy greater seclusion?"

"Yea, father," she answered, meekly. "He willeth that I abide as I am."

And then she told him the story of the night before.

The old priest breathed a sigh. "I thank God that He hath given thee this showing," he answered. "In sooth I have prayed much, too, for a light on this matter and it hath seemed to me, dear child, that an' He so willeth this thing He will make it to come to pass in His own way and in His own good time, and not in accordance with thy willing, that there may be nought of thine own choice in that which befalleth thee. May His grace go with thee, my dear daughter, for thy heart hath uttered a good word, and of a surety He will ever have from thee that which is most excellent."

So it fell out that on Easter morning, a week later, when Sir Nicholas the chaplain stepped round to the anchorage window after saying Mass, he found due access to the holy woman who had just been standing beside him at the empty tomb.

"Dear mother," he said, "what spiritual flower hast thou for me this happy day?"

"I have a new anchorhold for thee," she cried, and her voice was full of gaiety. "All its four walls are love, and love dwelleth in its midst."

"Through one of its windows thou takest and through one thou givest," he plunged in eagerly. "And the one looketh upon God," he said, "and the other on the world."

"Yea," she answered,—"but nay, both windows look upon God."

He noted the thrill of ecstasy in her voice. "Holy mother," he cried, "thou hast had a showing of God's Love. I pray thee that thou wilt tell me what thou hast learnt that I may preach it to the world." He held his breath waiting for the answer.

"Yea, I will tell thee," she replied, and then added meekly, "and so God give me the grace."

Chapter XIV

Wanton Kate

ATE THE WANTON hovered on the outskirts of the village like an unquiet spirit, albeit that she possessed a body—a befitting habitation for the kind of spirit that fights shy of places where humanity foregathers in the family circle in homes besprinkled with the parson's holy water, and house-warmed with the prayers and blessing of holy Mother Church. Wanton Kate was in a direful bad way: famished and exhausted, and likely to remain so. Had the twinkling lights in the village down in the hollow betokened a town or city Kate would have found the wherewithal to earn her shameful bread, but Kate had already sampled the moral calibre of the villagers in a rustic from whom she had begged an alms. She had begged at the parsonage also and received a rebuff. Sir Simon, the parson, was a man of rigid views and had a short way with erring femininity, and Kate's demeanour carried nothing either of repentance or of shame in it. She felt it to be futile to soil with her sore and bleeding feet the dust of this righteous village where she would only get cast out, or worse still, detained and made to do penance in a white sheet in the square-towered church yonder. She sat down on the roadside, on the stone rim that encircled a well. She had no particular use for the despised nectar. It was hunger that tore her to pieces with its fangs. She gathered her tattered finery close about her for the wind was chill and the gay-coloured silken rags were but a poor protection, immodesty contributing to their scantiness. She shivered and lifted her big,

washy eyes to the hills, fortuitously. They were the only living feature in her mask-like face, with its coatings of artifice obliterating
the original scheme like the distemper covering up a fresco. The
mouth possessed none of the curves formed either by laughter or
by pain. It was a gash outlined in red, hard set between the straight
downward lines in her hollow cheeks. Wanton Kate had done all
that lay within the devil that inhabited her to throw off the human
and assume the merely animal. Surely such a telltale countenance
had not been seen near a quiet country well-side since the days of
the stranger prophet who walked through Samaria.

She was not consciously looking towards the hills for help,
but as she did so she caught sight of the beacon light burning on
the tower of the fisherman's chapel. It recalled to her mind what
a child whom she had met on the road had told her. There was a
woman living walled-up there. A woman from the convent. Her
informant, not a very bright child, had told her the story in all
simplicity—the nuns had brought her there and put her in a cell
and walled her up, but they fed her every day with bread, plenty of
it, more than she wanted for she sometimes gave it away to beggars.
Recalling this story, an idea occurred to Kate. She had heard of
nuns being put under severe penance for heinous offences against
their vows. This woman had probably been guilty of something
exceptionally blatant, the more so the better for Kate's purpose.
If she climbed the hill she might find a kindred spirit, after all.
The desecrated nun could not, at all events, be shocked by her un-
lucky sister's antecedents, and in all probability she would be a
good-natured sort, and not averse, moreover, to come across one
of her own ilk; she might be willing to share her superabundant
prison fare in exchange for some news of the outside world not to
be gained from those who were permitted to approach her. At any
rate the idea was quite worth following up.

Kate the wanton rose and shook herself. She gathered her rags
round about her and set off in the direction of the beacon light,

which had reduced itself to a glimmer. It guided her accurately to the foot of the hill upon which stood the chapel of St. Catherine. She passed the yew tree, standing out, a ghastly shadow, in the darkness. It gave her the creeps. She shuddered. It was an awful punishment, this which had fallen upon this other woman. She must have had a fine fling to incur it, Kate reckoned, with a curious mixture of envy and compassion. She wondered how long ago it had happened. Well—at any rate they fed her, that was something.

She crept up the ascending path, cautiously. There were dead people buried near!—Ugh! It was better to die of hunger than to be cooped up there. She could now see the dark outline of the anchorhold, and approaching nearer she made out the path leading to the little window. It was too dark to see the neat flower-beds and well-trimmed hedge. She crept up furtively to the window and made a low, hissing sound, and followed it with an expression which might be rendered in the idiom of the reader's period as "Hi, you there!"

The answer was some little time in coming. Then a rather startled voice asked, "Who is it?"

The tones betrayed a certain amount of apprehension. It was not in this manner that the holy mother anchoress was accustomed to be saluted. A midnight call, of itself, was nothing out of the ordinary, for the holy recluse's prayers were ever in request for the dying.

Kate's answer was in words to this effect—she used a vernacular which can only be expressed by a translation into the modern equivalent.

"Say—give us a bit o' bread, old sport, I'm near dead with hunger and the old cats down there won't give me a bite, drat 'em. They're too good for the likes o' me." She laughed harshly—"but you've been in trouble yourself so you won't be too good." She repeated the bitter laugh, and waited.

There was a movement within. One speaks of a person being "taken aback." The sound within, or perhaps the absence of sound, was that produced by a person being taken aback.

"What didst thou say?" the anchoress's voice said, perhaps a little sharply.

"Oh, all right, don't fluff thy feathers, my dear. I know all about the sort o' nun thou a't. I don't blame thee for having thy fling. I hadn't any vows to break when I went to the devil, or I daresay I'd have been like thee instead of begging my bread. Give me a bit if thou'st got it. I'm starving. Come along now, we're sisters." Again she gave a hideous laugh. Her tone was half insolent, half whining.

Behind the curtain there reigned a kind of accentuated silence. "If thou wilt wait a minute," the voice said at last, "I will find thee some food." The tones were even. The speaker was calm and un-ruffled. Very calm and *very* unruffled.

Kate made appropriate answer—always assuming that the woman within had been a boon companion of her own approved "set." Her spirits were rising and her comments on the world in general are really not worth translating. A few minutes later a corner of the curtain was lifted and there was thrust out a loaf of fresh bread and a bowl of dried fruit. A cup of water followed. Then the curtain was quickly dropped into its place.

Kate grabbed the food. "God bless thee," she said, and fortu-nately the process of devouring it kept her more or less silent. It was excellent bread, and the dried fruit was quite good eating. She brought out a remark from time to time. "I guess thou'st played round a bit," she observed again to paraphrase her idiom, "before the game was up. Did they make thee stand in the church in a white thing and hold a candle before they put thee in here?" she added facetiously.

"Yes." The answer came slowly, and in a very low tone.

"Drat 'em!" Kate said, with real kindness. "I guess thoughthou wert a pretty highflyer—an out and out wrong 'un, like me. Now, say, weren't it so, *Sister*?" The harsh, metallic laugh followed the last word.

"Thou must pray for me," the voice inside replied, "for I am a very sinful woman."

Kate found herself slightly at a loss. She was unaccustomed to penitence.

"Not worse than me?" she suggested, well-manneredly.

"Yes; much worse."

Kate the wanton gave a low whistle, and superadded a profane word, which, however, carried no weight of intention. She considered for a moment. "Art thou sorry?" she asked. Her tones had likewise become lowered, and there was no harsh laugh.

"Yea, I have been a sinful woman, but I am penitent."

"Look here," said Kate the wanton, "just pop me into thy prayers, will 'ee?"

"Yea, and thou wilt go on praying for me," the anchoress said.

"I've not been praying for thee," Kate retorted, with swift honesty.

"Yea," came the answer. "When I gave thee food, thou saidst, 'God bless thee,' and—He blessed me."

"If thou'rt as sorry as all that," Kate said practically, "they ought to let thee out."

"No," the anchoress said, "I'm here to escape temptation."

"I suppose it is the wickedest sin," Kate said, meekly enough. Her voice had become almost gentle.

"Nay," the other voice answered, warmly, "pride is the wickedest sin."

There came a break in her voice. The anchoress was weeping bitterly.

Kate the wanton heard the sound and something hard melted inside her heart. Her thoughts fled to her first lover; to her mother, long dead; to a kitten that she had loved as a child, and a sudden tenderness flowed into her soul. She was seized with a longing to drag back the curtain and peep within. And then with a queer sense of the unseemliness of such an act. With a strange feeling of distance, of desire, of the wakening in her soul of something that had long slept there, she crept quietly away. Something had happened. After years spent in the slavery of her passions wanton Kate had experienced once again the pure delight of love.

Chapter XV

The Last Rood

ODIVA HAD DONE a lovely bit of thinking on the holy mystery of the Nativity, and she had come by a ghostly showing which she was anxious to report to the holy mother anchoress who had instructed her in this pious art of thinking on holy things in a tidy and methodical manner. Godiva was now sixteen years old, a growing maiden with a fine, thoughtful face, still given to dreaming, but with her dreams pointed and made fruitful of solid virtue through the ghostly counselling of her friend, the expert in the anchorhold. Ten years is a reasonable time in which to make an expert in any art, and the occupant of the anchorhold might be said to have stuck to her subject pretty well.

Perpetua had long since given up predicting a change in the anchoress's point of view. Her pessimism sought refuge in allusions to spiritual pride, and the fall to which it is a prelude. The fame of the anchoress's piety and spiritual enlightenment had spread, and there were many distinguished visitors to the parlour-window in these days. The idle folk had thinned themselves out by a natural process, a feeling of awe for one who gave counsel even to persons of ecclesiastical rank keeping them from importuning the holy lady with the minutiæ of their own lives. Godiva still continued to visit the anchoress regularly, for she had come to think seriously of the higher call and it was eminently the holy woman's business to lead her soul on to the spiritual heights towards which it was heading.

Godiva's visits to the anchorhold were big splashes of colour in the drab of her everyday life. To the holy mother she confided all those shy inmost feelings of her heart that she could not even have spoken of to Sir Nicholas himself, understanding though he had been, and her firm friend ever since the great day when he had rendered her the signal service of introducing her to the anchoress. Sir Nicholas had departed a year or more ago, to join the Order of the Black Friars, and he was now Fra Nicholas and wore the white habit and black cloak of his order. It was said that he had a great message to give the world, and that when his training was over and he went forth preaching he would scathe the heretics who infested the land spitting out the venom of their false doctrine. The pilgrims who called at the anchorage brought news of the scholar-friar to Dame Catherine, who recounted it to Godiva. It evidently gave her great joy.

The secret desire of Godiva's heart was to enter the convent in the capacity of extern sister. She sometimes visited old Sister Felicity, who had become crippled with rheumatism and she found that the life appealed to her. She had spoken of her desire to Father Nicholas, with all due diffidence, and he had not only encouraged her in the idea but had even suggested that her vocation might be that of a choir sister—one who led a contemplative life in the enclosure. Godiva, however, failed to be attracted by this higher honour. Her leaning lay towards the humble extern sisters who waited on those in the cloister—and also on the holy recluse in her anchorhold. Of all the people in the world the extern sisters at the convent alone looked on the features of the holy mother. They not only waited upon her needs, kindled her fire and cooked her food, but they also had the joy of speaking with her about their souls at the inner uncurtained window.

Godiva had often and often ached to ask Felicity to describe the holy mother's appearance to her, but she possessed a delicate sense of what a verbally gifted later age has called "playing the game," and she felt in some subconscious way that it would hardly be doing so to use Felicity's eyes for the purpose. Felicity, in her capacity of serving-woman, was, so to speak, the custodian of a king's secret—a position, by the way, which, as the reader will recall, she was eminently fitted to fill. She spoke but shyly of her vocation to the anchoress herself. Godiva was not entirely in her own confidence as to the reason of this reticence. Once she had spoken of her dream of becoming a lay sister, and the invisible lady had gently twitted her with the bygone incident of the broken pitcher. Alas, for Godiva's claim to domestic qualifications. In the convent kitchen she would be constantly putting the anchoress to the trouble of obtaining a "miracle" on her behalf.

Godiva sped her way towards the anchorage eagerly. She had hurried through her domestic work, to the imminent peril of the crockery, and now, when she arrived at the foot of the hill, she pulled up suddenly before the yew tree and stood gazing at it blankly. Upon its trunk there was fixed the white cross that warned would-be visitors that the anchoress was in retreat. It was an absolutely unexpected set-back. The recluse lady seldom had resort to a stricter retirement in these days. She was at the beck and call of those who desired her prayers, albeit that the busybodies found small encouragement. Godiva stood stock still; and so did her heart. It might mean that the holy mother was ill. That terrible thing had happened before, and Godiva had lived through periods of agony lest she should be destined never to hear again the voice behind the curtain. They could tell her up at the convent what had happened. Godiva turned and made a beeline across the meadows for the imposing building which she hoped might one day be her home.

She reached the convent panting and pale-faced, but the portress quickly relieved her fears. The holy mother had only retired into stricter seclusion for the time being to "do penance for her sins." That was the message she had bidden them give to those who enquired.

The Lady Prioress chanced to cross the hall as the portress was imparting her information. She smiled very cordially on the girl. "Well, Godiva," she said, "and when art thou coming to stay with us?"

Godiva blushed. It was more direct than anything that the Lady Prioress had ever said before. "I'm learning to be useful, Reverend Mother," she replied. "I can cook and wash, and scrub——"

"And pray?" the Prioress suggested. "Methinks there is more of Mary than of Martha about thee, Godiva."

Godiva blushed yet more deeply. It was partly with discomfiture. The Prioress had hinted before that the choir might be the place for her, but she felt no attraction for the enclosed life, much as she admired its most approved exponent.

"Well, child," the Lady Prioress said, kindly, "thy place is waiting for thee wherever it be, and whenever thou art ready to come."

It was glorious hearing for Godiva; she longed to rush and tell the anchoress. It was hard lines indeed that she should have selected the present time for doing penance for her sins—her sins! She went home to think over the Lady Prioress's words, and it might be to act upon them—without, indeed, advice from the anchorhold window; but, on the other hand, it would be a delightful piece of news for the holy mother when she came out of retreat.

On the seventh day of the anchoress's strict seclusion there came a visitor to the anchorage who was not deterred by the sight of the white cross for the simple reason that she had not been told of its meaning. She was a woman poorly but respectably dressed in the rough garments worn by the women who worked in the fields. She was scarcely built that way, but she walked with a swinging stride that suggested at any rate strength of purpose. She had already paid one visit—it had been to the parsonage—and she was now on her way to tell the inmate of the cell against the church wall how it had resulted.

Wanton Kate, for it was she and no other, found her way to the curtained window. She was too eagerly occupied with her thoughts to note the well-kept approach to the "penal erection." She set herself down on the visitors' bench and repeated her call of the previous occasion. It was immediately answered from within.

"It's all right," the visitor said, and probably she added some genial appellation equivalent to "old pal"—one has the greatest difficulty in rendering wanton Kate as she appeared to her hostess, except by the frank use of anachronisms. "I haven't come to beg. Can't 'ee pull that curtain back and have a look at me? They won't let thee, I suppose. Well—I'm honest. I've earned honest wages this whole week—in the fields; and do ye know why? I'm going to show 'em that a woman the likes o' thee and me can turn and go straight if she likes, and when I can show 'em six months of it belike they'll let thee out and give thee a chance, too. I've been to the parson and told him so." Kate's tones were sturdy and triumphant.

"And what did he say?" the voice of the listener asked.

"He looked as if he didn't understand at first," Kate said, "so I told him how the nuns had walled thee in because thou'd been a bad 'un. 'Art thou sure?' says he. 'Yes, Thy Reverence,' says I, 'for she told me so herself.' 'Well,' says he, 'I know that the good sisters are very close about their affairs and they haven't been very frank with me over this business. I never dreamt that that was the case. What dost thou want me to do?' he says. 'I want thee to tell 'em to let her out,' says I. 'They wouldn't listen to me,' he says, 'but I'll do what I can. Thou art a brave girl, and I'll pray that thou may keep straight.' 'Never fear,' says I. So that's the top and bottom of it, so cheer up, old hide-away, I don't doubt but he'll speak to the nuns and they'll give thee another chance."

"I don't think that he will," the interior lady answered, "but he evidently believed what thou saidst. That is a thing to be full thankful for. I thank thee, dearest sister, with all my heart."

There was so much joy in her voice that Kate was touched to the depths of her recently recovered soul.

She pressed her face close to the curtain. "I mean to keep to it—always," she whispered. "I've got to loathe the other—just like thee."

The curtain against which her face was pressing suddenly ceased to yield. There was a face on the other side and the anchoress was kissing her through the white linen cross.

She left the anchorage to set out on her twenty-mile trudge to the scene of her new activities, her soiled, broken-nailed hands wrung together and the tears in her eyes, which had once more regained the divine image. Her stride was as determined as ever.

In her cell the anchoress was saying a *Te Deum*, for she had raised the purchase money of the last rood of the field containing the treasure. Along the road there was approaching a queer figure—that of a wandering minstrel, fantastically garbed in red and blue, accompanied by an exceedingly ancient mongrel dog. Across the meadows from the convent a girl was hastening, accompanied by one of the convent sisters. It was Godiva, acting *ex-officio*, for she had entered the convent that morning as a lay sister and she was on her way to visit the anchoress.

When Kate and the jongleur met on the highway, they exchanged a cordial greeting. Fiddlemee was an old acquaintance of more prosperous days—a fact which, however, cast no slur upon his reputation. Kate had sized him up and left him alone. He had religion, although he was a jongleur, and a funny, fantastic fellow, and somehow he reminded her of the friars—a class of churchmen who appealed to erring, church-shy folk like herself.

As they walked along in company she found herself telling him her story, and he became mightily interested when she told him about the walled-up nun. Kate described her first visit in detail, her voluble tongue repeating the conversation in the "she says, I says" manner of her class.

"And she didn't deny it?" the listener said.

"No," Kate answered. "I thought just for a minute like that she was going to, but she didn't—and then afterwards she told me, right out, that she was a sinful woman, just like me—no, worse nor me, it was, she said. I'm glad that she didn't get up on her perch, for I thought she was going to—just at first."

The jongleur's bright eyes sparkled and his face crumpled up into a gleeful expression. He made a grab at his lute and proceeded to strike a resonant chord.

Kate glared him into silence. She was not going to permit ribald comment on her story. "*Laus Deo!*" the jongleur said, and swung the instrument back over his shoulder. Kate continued her narrative. She told of her resolution, and of her finding work in the fields, and her subsequent visit to Sir Simon. She had no reason to complain of her companion's levity. He listened intently, every now and again he swept his fingers lightly over the strings of "Orpheus" and as she described her interview with the priest, he repeated his *Laus Deo*, under his breath. He had become madder than ever, Kate thought, yet she was able to tell him her story as she could not have told it to another.

When they reached the cross-roads their journeys lay in different directions. "Fare thee well," the jongleur said. "Go on digging in the fields, for remember, the Kingdom of Heaven is like unto a treasure hidden in a field, so look well at the stubble that thou turnst up for thou mayest turn up the Kingdom of Heaven." He felt for the lute, unconsciously. His face had lighted up as it did when he was about to burst out into a mad ditty, but he only repeated his "*Laus Deo!*"

When the other had gone on her way he sat himself down on a milestone with the lute on his knee and his hand hovering over the strings. The dog watched him anxiously. Suddenly he sprang up. "Come, Flipkin," he cried. "We will turn back and be holy pilgrims for the nonce." The dog dropped his tail. He had a doggy instinct that being a holy pilgrim would mean extra weariness. To retrace one's steps on a journey is mortifying to the instinct which bids one follow one's nose.

So it fell out that they tramped back together as far as the meadows leading up to the convent and the beacon chapel.

Chapter XVI

The Vision

MEANWHILE, whilst Kate and her companion journeyed together, Godiva was approaching the anchorage. It was hard indeed to believe this wonderful ending to her story—that she was really and truly to enter the magic precincts and actually to look upon the countenance of the invisible lady. It seemed like a hark back to the fairy tale of her childhood, recalling somehow the glamour of that occasion when she and Father Nicholas had sought the anchorhold together. They had approached it then in the ordinary way, but now, she was to be one of those privileged to enter the other way. She felt extraordinarily like the Godiva of six years ago. Life had not ceased to be a fairy tale.

At the convent she had been greeted with the glad news that the holy mother would be out of retreat, and that Godiva might herself carry to her the tidings of her entry into the religious life, as was befitting in the case of the one who had taken the young dreamer in hand and guided her desire to the everlasting hills. How near heaven had seemed during the precious hours that she had passed at the little parlour-window. Now she would receive her ghostly counsel in an even more intimate way, for—oh, wonderful thought! there would be no curtain.

Her companion was a cheery and garrulous soul, taking more after Felicity than Perpetua. Their basket of provisions contained some cheese, and the sister told Godiva how some morsels of the dainty would certainly go to the mouse of whom the anchoress had made a pet. So cunning had the creature become that he would pop out of his hole, so the mother had told them, when he heard the key grating in the lock, associating it with meal-time, and particularly cheese.

She rattled on, Godiva found no occasion to answer, or even to listen. She continued to enjoy her thoughts. The beloved spot was wrapped in its old enchantment. In the distance she saw the figure of a woman leaving the anchorage window. Godiva wondered what her business had been. Poor soul! she was fain to pity her because she was one of those who had to approach that way—to sit without the curtained window talking with an invisible lady.

Her heart was beating violently when they reached the little gate which admitted them from the meadows into the churchyard. The sister thrust the key and the basket into her hands. "Thou canst let thyself in," she said, "whilst I go down to the tree and take the cross away, or we shall be keeping the visitors off." She was a beautifully matter-of-fact person. Godiva took the key. It was big and grim-looking—this sesame to her wonderland—the place where she would receive sweet showings of God's love from the one whose four happy walls kept away all intruders. Her hand trembled when she inserted it in the lock in the stout oak door. It turned with a loud grating sound—as loud and harsh as that made by the church door lock itself. Godiva suddenly felt as though she were committing an act of sacrilege.

There was one, however, to whom an even more unwarranted intrusion by no means appeared in that light. The infirm brown mouse who subsisted on the anchoress's largess, heard the portentous sound. He emerged from his hole and suggested to his cellmate by his presence that the necessities of this life are not, after all, things to be completely ignored. He was a patient little creature, and very quiet; he was accustomed, moreover, to the anchoress's fits of preoccupation. He simply sat there and waited, fixing her with his bright eyes.

The Vision

Godiva pushed the door open and entered. She found herself in a narrow apartment. There was a fair-sized aperture in the opposite wall with a wide ledge like a buttery-hatch. Beyond it she caught a glimpse of the inner chamber. The supreme moment had arrived. A sudden shyness overtook her, mingling with the throbbing joy in her heart; and at that moment she heard the sound of the anchoress's voice. There was someone there speaking with her! There had been no one at the parlour-window, nor in sight even, save the departing woman. What could it mean? The feeling of intrusion gripped hold of Godiva afresh. Yet she was impelled, almost involuntarily, to draw closer to the window. She now obtained a view of the cell. The sun was shining through the window opposite, making the wide white cross on the drawn curtain a patch of golden radiance. Shafts of silver light crossed the cell from the holes, up near the roof which gave light and ventilation to the apartment. One of these fell obliquely across a figure standing in the centre of the cell. It missed the face, clothing the shoulders and lower part in its radiance. But the face had a radiance of its own which matched the other—nay, surpassed it. Godiva stepped backward, still clutching her basket. It was a smiling face and the eyes were cast down, regarding someone who presumably lay prostrate at the feet of the apparition. The anchoress would be invisible in that posture, but Godiva was not thinking of the anchoress whose vision she was sharing. No wonder the holy mother loved the four walls if it was thus that she was strengthened and comforted in her solitude!

> "The Master is so fair,
>   So sweet His smile to fallen men,
>   That those who meet Him unaware
>   Can never rest on Earth again."

Words that the anchoress had once repeated to her came into Godiva's mind in the brief moment in which she allowed herself to gaze on the privy sight. The next second an instinct made her turn and flee from the place which held the heavenly vision. The key was still in the lock. She closed the door very gently and waited there. She durst not turn the key for fear of the noise. She looked down at her hand for the basket. It was not there. She must have unconsciously let it go as she stood there looking. Godiva was empty-handed; and in her mind there was but one thought,

"The Master is so fair."

Her companion was approaching. "Hast thou not been in?" she asked.

"Yea, but I did not give her the basket," Godiva said. "I didn't like to disturb her."

"Never mind," the other said, "I'll see to it. Get thee on homeward and I will overtake thee."

So Godiva went slowly on her homeward way. She hastened her pace. She did not want the sister with her garrulous tongue to overtake her. She was thinking, thinking.

"Those who meet Him unaware can never rest on earth again." She had almost reached the convent gate by the time her companion overtook her. The Lady Prioress was walking in the garden. She caught sight of the new arrival and beckoned her to her. "Well, my child," she asked, and her voice was kind and encouraging, "How art thou liking thy first day with us?"

Godiva hesitated in replying.

"And dost thou still think that thou wouldst prefer to be a lay sister rather than stay in thy cell and think on God?" the Prioress said.

Godiva raised her eyes and met the mother's shrewd but gentle scrutiny.

"Mother," she said, "I think I would rather be the other kind and stay in my cell."

"And why?"

"Because—because," Godiva said, "I think might learn more about—about Him if there were no one else there. If I were all alone, and He were all alone."

"The anchoress hath told thee this?" the mother said.

"Nay," Godiva answered. "I saw her not. She was—praying and so I came away."

A look of some wonder came into the listener's face.

"Godiva," she said. "Hast thou realised what this step meaneth? It meaneth that thou wilt never leave the cloister—not even to visit the anchoress."

There was a pause. Then Godiva looked up.

"Yea, Mother," she said, huskily. "I understand."

"And thou art willing to enter now?" They were standing at the big doorway. Before them ran the long corridor leading to the cloister.

"Yes, Reverend Mother, I am willing," Godiva answered.

The Prioress placed her arm around the child and kissed her.

"Methought God meant it," she said.

Somewhere about that moment the jongleur and his dog were approaching the anchorage—by the back way, over the graves for they were not visitors in the ordinary sense—for that reason it was no matter that they avoided the warning sign on the tree over by the gate. They found themselves outside the anchorage, close by the door through which the anchoress's attendants visited her. The door over whose threshold the anchoress had passed ten years before—which had just been recrossed by an eavesdropper fleeing from a vision.

It was a rough stone step, once pressed by the dainty feet of the anchoress. Fiddlemee the jongleur knelt down upon his red knee and upon his blue knee, and kissed it.

Flipkin, his dog, shook his aged body and turned round. "Come along," he appeared to be saying. "That's over anyhow."

Chapter XVII

The King's Highway

IR SIMON, the parish priest, was plodding his way up the road leading to the convent with a view to securing a side of the famous bacon cured on the convent farm and supplied to himself on special terms. Sir Simon disliked calling on the lady prioress. He had strong prejudices to match his somewhat limited perceptions, and he cherished a prejudice against nuns whilst the length of his perceptions fell considerably short of the "include" ideal, so the convent and its off-shoot, the anchorhold, were both of them irritants that formed an excellent substitute for the hairshirt, a garment to the wearing of which honest Sir Simon never pretended to aspire. The worthy parish priest hugged a dual grievance against the nuns, one being that they occupied themselves too much with the affairs of the world, such as rightly belonged to the other sex, and the other the familiar objection to "a herd of women shut up together and doing no good." Sir Simon and the lady prioress existed on what are generally known as terms of civility. Her bacon was extremely good eating, and the terms were made reasonable to one of his holy calling so Sir Simon behaved with all due courtesy to the lady superior, who was also, by the way, a very superior lady, and a firm ruler in spite of her advanced years. It was a sore point with Sir Simon that the prioress kept her own spiritual director, a holy Franciscan friar, also far advanced in years. Once a year only the nuns were required to be shriven by their parish priest. Another sore point was the lady anchoress. Sir Simon had no truck with the anchorhold himself, but the best curate he had ever had had fallen under the influence of the inmate of the anchorhold, being a constant visitor at her window, and had contracted spiritual fidgets and gone off to the Black Friars, with a special dispensation from the bishop, and Sir Simon had been left with many parochial and extra-parochial activities on his hands which succeeding chantry chaplains declined to consider as part of their duties.

The anchoress was very much in Sir Simon's mind on the present occasion on account of a peculiar visit he had received not long back from a woman who declared herself to be a penitent. This incident had made a great impression on the mind of Sir Simon. The woman in question had made a most extraordinary statement concerning the anchoress. Obviously there was no occasion to credit a story told by a woman of her ilk but there had been an amazing convincingness about the roughly-clad woman who had shown him her torn and blistered hands and told him that she had been keeping herself by honest labour, and then begged him to take it as a proof that the woman shut up in the cell against the church would do likewise if granted her freedom. She had stood there before him—this strange woman, with tears of entreaty in her eyes, and she had declared that the anchoress was likewise a penitent—as penitent as herself—she, the anchoress, had told her so herself when she gave her her own supper. And she had implored him to plead with the nuns on her behalf. That, of course, was preposterous. There was no question of the anchoress being an involuntary prisoner, but Sir Simon wondered how much truth there might be behind. Had the holy anchoress indeed got a past to atone for? And did the nuns know it? He would dearly like to find out the rights of the case. The lady prioress had never been expansive to him about her affairs, except in so far as they related to bacon and cheese and chicken-rearing. She might well be wilfully misleading him, along with the others, over this business. He certainly could not count on pumping the truth out of her. Her assistant, Dame Anneys, was far more likely to be accessible in that way. Dame Anneys looked after the farm department and was not without interest in the things of the outside world. Sir Simon felt more at his ease with her than with the paramount lady.

Upon reaching the convent the parson was conducted to the parlour. Dame Anneys happened to be there with her superior, and the latter bade her remain as a side of bacon was the objective of the visit.

Sir Simon, having duly bestowed his blessing, enquired politely after the health of the inmates of the convent. "And the Lady Anchoress," he added, "I trust she is also in health."

It was unusual for Sir Simon to include the lady of the anchorhold in his enquiries, he generally ignored her, with more or less intention. "I met someone who knew her formerly, the other day," he observed, "who spoke of her former mode of life, very different from the present."

Sir Simon fondly believed that he was making his observation in quite a casual manner.

Dame Anneys looked up quickly from the place where her hands reposed beneath her scapular. She had not been long at the convent having been transferred from another house, and she was curious as to the antecedents of the lady in the anchorhold whose facilities for combining sanctity with an agreeable accessibility to the outside world were a not unnatural irritant to the human nature which remains human nature even in a convent. Curiosity was a weakness which the prioress severely discouraged, and Dame Anneys had never dared make too many enquiries. Dame Catherine had become Dame Catherine on the day she entered the anchorhold, what she had been in the world was not a matter to be enquired about.

"The lady anchoress occupied a very high social position before she entered religion," the mother prioress said. She noted the manner in which Sir Simon delivered his "casual" observation and wondered what lay behind it.

"I suppose thou wert unacquainted with her in those days," Sir Simon went on, "she must have led a very gay life."

Dame Anneys pricked up her ears, which habitually failed to take a hint from their monastic covering.

"Dame Catherine renounced great possessions in order to gain the Kingdom of Heaven," the Prioress replied. There was a stiffness in her manner that piqued Sir Simon. He took it to be a reticence of a secretive kind, and Sir Simon's was the type of mind which regards all reserve as secretiveness—it was the defect of his virtue of honesty, a virtue which was making his attempt at diplomacy so remarkably clumsy on the present occasion.

"That kind of life," he observed, "hath grave dangers, and few escape them, but she is certainly making ample amends."

The innuendo was unmistakable. Dame Anneys fixed her near-set eyes on Sir Simon and ached to hear more, but her superior was minded otherwise. "Thy Reverence hath paid us a great compliment in seeking a supply of our pork," she said, suavely. "Dame Anneys will take it to herself, soothly, for she hath charge of the dairy," and she turned the conversation deftly on to cheese and the pickling of fish, and such matters. Dame Anneys, for all the compliment, looked as though she would have preferred to continue the other conversation, but she would get her chance later on when Sir Simon visited the dairy to make his selection, and that without the chilling presence of a superior who regarded even the most innocent piece of chatter as scandal.

"I am but a Martha," she observed, deprecatingly, as she led her client to the farm premises. "I expect thou wilt be comparing me with the Mary of whom we were speaking just now."

"Dost thou mean the anchoress?" Sir Simon asked.

"Yea," Dame Anneys said. "She is in sooth a Mary Magdalen, but perhaps I were wrong to say that as so many take the Magdalen to mean that one might have been a sinner."

Sir Simon rubbed his chin. He felt at home with Dame Anneys, and he was not unwilling to recount the story, strange in itself, of wanton Kate's visit and extraordinary request. He considered. Dame Anneys unlocked the dairy door. "I must show thee my cheeses," she said, "the mother anchoress hath a great liking for cheese, although it must be poor fare compared with that which she were used to, as doubtless thy friend did tell thee."

"'Twas no friend of mine but a woman that was a wanton," Sir Simon answered.

Dame Anneys locked the dairy door on the inside. "So many come in that should not," she observed. She made no further allusion to the cheeses.

When she returned to the parlour half-an-hour later the Prioress observed that Sir Simon had been some time choosing his side of bacon. Dame Anneys admitted that he had been so. She had nothing further to tell her superior, for had not the latter taught her not to repeat the tales that came to her ears, and in this case the mother superior knew it already. Furthermore she might put Anneys herself under obedience not to pass the story on where it might be duly appreciated. So Dame Anneys held her peace—or rather entrenched it within a wordy account of Sir Simon's opinion of the white cheese as opposed to the yellow.

As for Sir Simon, he wended his way homeward. He had developed a thirst which Dame Anneys had omitted to offer to assuage. Never mind, the Cross Keys, the tavern on the roadside opposite, where the anchoress's visitors refreshed themselves, was quite handy and Master Hubert, the taverner, would appreciate a visit from the parson.

Master Hubert, however, appeared to be in a downcast mood which defied even the cheeriness of Sir Simon's genial greeting.

"How go I?" he repeated, "how should a man go that is ruined and done for."

"What dost thou mean?" Sir Simon queried.

"Why, hast thou not heard?" the other answered. "The sheriff's man from Newstowe hath just ridden by and he telleth me that the scheme for taking the high road straight along through the village hath been permitted at last, and within a few months no traveller will pass my doors save those who seek the cove or the beacon chapel."

The news took Sir Simon pretty well off his feet. The diverting of an ancient highway is not an every-day occurrence, albeit that the present condition of things was one that cried out for the alteration which was at length to be undertaken. It had been for years under discussion in the courts of law but no one ever dreamt of the thing being brought to a conclusion.

Sir Simon did his best to console the luckless taverner whose loss would be his own gain, since the backwater village would now be placed in the mid-current, so to speak.

"Well, well," quoth he, "there will be the pilgrims to the anchor-hold left, at any rate."

But Hubert shook his head and refused to be comforted. "There will be no pilgrims to the anchorhold," he prophesied, glumly, "when the high road passeth no longer this way. 'Tis lying near the high road that hath gained the anchorhold its visitors." He was applying an axiom to the anchoress's spiritual traffic with which the commercial expert would have fully concurred. Sir Simon drank his ale and left mine host as glum as he had found him.

So bubbling over with the great news was Sir Simon that when he caught sight of the convent chaplain approaching slowly he went to the length of stopping to speak to the old man who had gained a reputation for living in the third heaven and passing over the elementary necessities of life as beside the point. Sir Simon made an effort to import his news so that it might find a foothold in the soft substance of the old visionary's brain. He put it facetiously.

"The good ladies up yonder," he observed, wagging his head in the direction of the convent, and of the anchorage, "will enjoy a little more seclusion in the future, methinks. They be going to divert the King's highway for that special purpose and take it round by my church instead. In a very short time there will be no more pilgrims to ride past the anchorhold and disturb the holy mother."

The old man looked up. A gentle flicker of interest crossed his face. "So it hath come," he said, "in God's good time, and in God's own way."

The old monk whose habitual domicile was said to be the third heaven was looking at the information in his own way—an inverted presentment of the case. For him the King's highway had been swept out of its course as an accessory to the main scheme in operation up at the anchorhold. There was nothing surprising in the circumstance; was it not the King's highway?

"I doubt me if the old dotard hath taken in what I said," Sir Simon observed to himself. "I wonder what a shrewd woman like yon Dame Anneys maketh of such a confessor. Beshrew me, but doth she make confession to him that she hath talked scandal concerning the holy mother anchoress, he will but answer, 'It hath come in God's time and in His way.'" He chuckled to himself at his somewhat profane jest, and hastened his steps towards home to impart his news into the more intelligent ears of Mrs. Martha.

Chapter XVIII

The Book of Roger de Worde

MASTER ROGER de Worde, gentleman and clerk of Oxford, had made a book. He had written out the treasures of his mind in fair script, and the book of Roger de Worde needed nothing but a binding to make it fit for the library shelf. But Master Roger had no intention that his book should remain an isolated work of one edition consisting of one copy. It contained a message to the world—no other message than that which Fra Nicholas, the Black Friar, who was fast leaping into fame as a preacher, was delivering up and down the country. The friar's glowing words and soul-inspiring revelation of Divine Love had taken the hearts of men by storm in an age when many had grown sick with the overwhelming problems of the day. Fra Nicholas had proved a hammer for the Lollards, and it was for the confounding of Lollardry that Roger de Worde had written his book, based on the life-giving doctrine of the Black Friar whose orthodoxy and loyalty to Holy Church were beyond reproach. Master Roger being a gentleman as well as a clerk, had first insisted that the book should be written by the friar himself, but Fra Nicholas had put away the suggestion. He had made a book once upon a time, he told the other, and if it had not fallen out by the mercy of God that the manuscript had got destroyed he might at this moment be answerable for the loss of numberless souls, for it was written in the dark spirit of revolt, and the truth it contained had been diluted and contaminated with self-complacency. He had laid his pen aside and determined to use rather the gift of speech, so Roger was welcome to the task. Moreover Fra Nicholas explained, the message was not of his own direct receiving but had been passed on to him by one whose identity he had promised to keep secret—a holy woman learned in ghostly lore who lived recluse in an anchorhold. She had received the irresistible "showing" and had handed it to him—instructed him in the various ways of understanding it—so that it was in sooth no more his than Roger's—that was to say it was as much at Roger's disposal for propagation as his own. So Roger de Worde sat down and made his book.

Whilst his task was in progress Fra Nicholas was called away to a House of Studies belonging to his Order in the North of England. He was vastly interested in Roger's work, and sent word from the monastery that when the treatise was completed if Master de Worde would carry it thither the brothers in the scriptorium would make a number of fair copies for circulation in quarters where it would do good to souls warping towards Lollardry.

In the course of time the great day arrived when Roger de Worde wrote the last syllable in his script. The book was finished. Soothly it was a work that any author might be proud of. Roger had a fluent pen and a happy choice of words in which to clothe his ideas. He was a poet, moreover, and missed nothing of the beauty of his message. He surveyed the script with all complacency; and being a gentleman at large with no lack of means he set forth on his journey to the North carrying with him the precious volume which, after receiving the father prior's approval, was to be increased and multiplied for the perusal of the world at large, like the works of the great Walter Hilton, or Thomas of Kempen. No wonder Master de Worde felt fairly satisfied with himself. He made good haste on his journey, and like many who do so, the result was less speed. Thus when Roger had covered about half the distance between himself and the place where his work was to break in upon the wondering minds of the black brethren, he discovered that his horse was giving out and needed a rest. White Star was a special favourite of his master's and Roger had no mind to treat his friend hardly, so, not without much inward chafing, he arranged to stop at the inn in the village through which he was passing at the time. The inn was newly built, and the landlord, Master Hubert, told his guest how he had removed from his former hostelry which had stood on the highway, where it had looped round towards the cliff. The making of the new road had meant a saving of perhaps three-quarters of a mile.

Master Hubert, mindful for the entertainment of his guest during the two days of his enforced sojourn, introduced him to the parson, Sir Simon. Sir Simon displayed much cordiality towards the distinguished stranger. Things were not so dead-alive as in the old days when the high road fought shy of the village, but Sir Simon was a genial soul and he dearly loved a gossip with someone from the outside world, so he invited Master de Worde to supper on the first evening of his arrival and did him very well both in matter of the produce from his own garden and the convent farm, where things flourished mightily under the eye of the Lady Prioress Anneys. The latter had become superior on the death of the old prioress which had occurred just about the time that they started to make the new road. Dame Anneys had not allowed the diversion of the traffic to affect the commerce of the convent farm, for she was a thoroughly efficient business-woman.

Master Roger, being a dreamer and a mystic, and several other things of the kind, was rather bored by Sir Simon. He sat by the blazing hearth after supper and when at length an opportunity came initiated his host into the absorbing secret of his book, which he had brought over with him thinking the parson might be interested.

Sir Simon took the fairly-written script in his hands. He opened it and perused a page at a hazard whilst the author sat in warm contentment and waited for his comment. The comment was characteristic.

"It hath not got a binding," Sir Simon observed. "Why ever dost thou not get it bound?"

Master Roger was just a little bit ruffled at the inconsequent criticism.

"I had no time," he said. "Doubtless they will bind it for me at the Monastery. They are to make some three score fair copies of the work," he added, with a slight access of learned clerk into his manner.

"It looketh a poor thing as it stands," Sir Simon said bluntly, contemplating the MS. with something akin to contempt.

"Well, a poor thing it will have to remain," Master Roger returned, tartly, "for it be too late now to do anything. I don't suppose there is anyone in this place who knoweth a book when he seeth one, let alone bindeth such."

Sir Simon rubbed his chin meditatively. The scornful rejoinder was entirely without sting to his simple nature.

"I have heard say that the anchoress up at the chapel bindeth books for a pastime," he observed, "and that not badly considering. She might bind it for thee. I don't doubt me but she'd be pleased enough to have the doing of it."

Master Roger demurred. "Hast thou seen any of her work?" he enquired, suspiciously, with doubt rampant in his tone.

Sir Simon admitted that he had not. He had very little traffic with the anchoress, but the simple folk sometimes took their broken chattels up to the anchorhold for her to mend. She appeared to be deft with her fingers and was always ready to undertake a job. She was a harmless soul. They got her to pray for their sick cows, and they looked upon her as a sort of white witch.

"How cometh she by the book-binding?" Roger asked.

"Oh, she binds the nuns' books," Sir Simon explained. "She belongeth to the convent, only they be mighty afraid of her, for it was put abroad that she had got affected towards Lollardry. The sisters attend to her needs but the prioress sees to it that they don't gossip at her window or take ghostly counsel, and by way of return she binds their books and mends their habits."

"Well," Master Roger said doubtfully, "I have no wish to see my book mishandled. I would rather be sure of how she doth the work first."

"I tell thee what," Sir Simon said, "suppose we give her some old book of mine and let her bind that, and if she doeth it all right she shall have the doing of thine. She worketh very quickly, I've been told."

He got up and went over and rummaged in a corner, and returned with a volume in his hand. It was a book of "færie gestes" for children, copied out in neat script, and containing illustrations remarkably vivid in colouring and conception. It possessed a tattered binding, but this Sir Simon ripped off. He surveyed the resplendent elves and goblins, creations of the age that gave the world the gargoyle, triumphantly.

"That will be just the thing," he commented. "My curate, who serveth the chantry chapel over against which the anchorhold is built, can take it over in the morning, and if she do it right away she can have thine in the afternoon."

He placed it on the table beside Master Roger's script. "They be much alike," he observed, sublimely oblivious of the quaintness of the observation, viewed from another standpoint. "Thou wilt be able to tell how the book will look. It seemeth to me a poor compliment to hand the likes of it as it stands to the prior." In the intervening years Sir Simon had got over his grudge against the Black Friars for stealing his best curate. Master de Worde had not mentioned the name of his friend at court, so the parson remained in ignorance of the connection between the book and the erstwhile Nicholas the chaplain.

Master Roger was beginning to see the thing from Sir Simon's practical, if limited point of view. It really might be more graceful to present the volume in a comely form; besides, a binding would give it a consummated character that might influence the censorship in the right direction.

Being youthful, Master de Worde now became possessed of the desire to get the suggestion carried out without delay. The same impetuosity that had ridden White Star to the detriment of his health caused him to express his intention of visiting the anchorhold there and then and enlisting the good services of its inmate.

"Tut, tut, man," Sir Simon said. "My curate will see to the matter for thee, and if thou goest up by noon thou wilt find the sample of the good soul's handicraft ready for thee to judge." And Master Roger was fain to accept the kindly and sensible offer.

It was, consequently, at noon on the following day that he found himself traversing the meadows that lay in the loop between the main road and the old disused thoroughfare that drew its grass-grown trail past the ascent upon which the chantry chapel stood.

What a desolate, neglected place it was! There was an air of other days about it that added to its dreariness. A ragged, untrimmed hedge, broken down in places, screened off the path leading to the anchorhold. The borders of the weed-grown path suggested that they had received attention at some bygone era. A few sturdy violets were throwing out their fragrance from the untended beds. The tide of life had indeed flowed away and left the anchorhold stranded high and dry. The gracefully-designed, mullioned parlour-window alone remained the same, its lower section curtained with a black curtain into which was inserted a wide white linen cross. The note of desolation struck Roger de Worde, though he had no comparison to make, never having visited the spot before. Dereliction was in the atmosphere, and Master Roger was sensitive to atmospheres. The birds alone seemed unaffected. Up in the trees they were twittering to one another, for it was nearing the feast of St. Valentine and the mating season was approaching. But birds have been known to sing on a battlefield.

Master de Worde hurried up to the window and rapped with his knuckles on the ledge. Something in Sir Simon's manner, even more than his actual words, had conveyed the impression to Roger that the inmate of the anchorhold was not a person with whom one need stand on ceremony. He answered the gentle and very prompt greeting from the other side of the curtain with directness that in no way savoured of deference to the holy woman's estate.

"Hast thou ready the book that Sir Simon the parson did send thee yestreen for to bind?" he enquired.

"I have it not quite ready to send away," the other replied, "it is still in my press, but I can take it out and show it to thee. His Reverence the chaplain did say that if so I had done the work passably there might be yet another book for me to bind. I will show thee what I have done."

A minute later a volume neatly bound in leather was thrust through the window for the visitor's inspection. Master de Worde examined it full carefully. The work might be pronounced to be excellent in every way. No possible exception could be taken either to material or workmanship.

Roger was delighted. He dived into his wallet and produced his precious script.

With extreme graciousness he explained to the woman within that the present work was one of the utmost importance, containing great lights on holy religion. He managed to convey, delicately, a hint that the binder of such a work might feel herself duly honoured, though of course he did not fail to offer her a reasonable price for her trouble, to be paid, if she wished it, in alms to the poor. He did not suggest that she might like to make herself acquainted with what had been written on Holy Religion although Sir Simon had said that the anchoress was not "entirely unlettered." The subtlety of its contents would undoubtedly be beyond her comprehension. Indeed he went to the length of telling her this, lest having heard that it was a work of unreckoned value, curiosity might move her to attempt to peruse its contents and thus waste valuable time.

"Thou shalt have it ready by this evening," the anchoress told him. She was as direct and business-like as himself. He had told her the dazzling fact that he was in sooth Master Roger de Worde, the scholar and mystic of Oxford, but this had apparently conveyed nothing beyond a sense of increased deference to the woman behind the curtain, as would naturally be the case.

"Well, I will leave it with thee," Master Roger said, "and I warn thee, good mother, do not waste time trying to make sense of the showing that it containeth for it requireth much spiritual subtlety to comprehend what hath been written here. 'Tis the same doctrine that is preached by one Fra Nicholas, of the Black Friars, which I have set forth therein."

"Then soothly it is full speedful and Christian," the anchoress replied. "I knew Fra Nicholas once upon a time, but it is a-many years since I have seen him. But I promise thee I will not waste time wrestling with the contents of thy book."

So Master de Worde left the anchorage reassured and in mighty good conceit with himself, withal.

The anchoress proved herself to be as good as her word. When Master Roger presented himself at the anchorage for a second time, soon after sunset, he found his book duly waiting for him in its binding. It would have been better for a few more hours in the press but if Master Roger promised not to handle it too freely before the glue dried, all would be well.

The corner of the curtain was withdrawn, and the craftswoman proceeded to hand over both the volumes committed into her care. They were bound in identical fashion, with not a pin to choose between the two. "I trust thou wilt find them to thy liking," the anchoress said. Like the worthy Sir Simon she evidently regarded the two from a standpoint which made them much of a muchness.

Master de Worde was more amused than piqued, on this occasion. He surveyed the second volume committed into his care dubiously. It would mean making another call at the rectory to restore it to its owner, and yet he could not well refuse to take it. He tactfully evolved a way out of the difficulty.

"Might it not make a pastime for thee to read these 'færie gestes'?" he suggested kindly. "Thou must sometimes need a little lightness to ease thy day."

"I thank thee," the anchoress answered, courteously, "but it so happeneth that I must ask leave of my ghostly director concerning the writings that I read—'tis in my rule—and it be so in these days that I but rarely have recourse to him for he is of a great age and full infirm, and seldom leaveth the convent."

Master de Worde smiled to himself at the simplicity of the reply. The "færie gestes" seemed to be destined to find a place in the same category as his book of revelations. He picked the neatly-bound volume up along with his own and placed the two in his wallet. Then he bade the inmate of the anchorage a courteous farewell, thanking her for her pains.

"Remember, good mother," he remarked, with much kindness, "thou wilt in sooth have had a hand in the making of a book that hath a great mission before it."

At the foot of the path Master de Worde remounted his horse, now sufficiently recovered from the effects of his unwonted exertions. He rode along the deserted loop-road thinking deeply of the future, and of the destiny of his *opus magnum*. It was not until he had ridden many miles that he realised that he had completely forgotten to ride back to the village and deliver over to Sir Simon his book of "færie gestes."

Chapter XIX

A Færie Geste

ASTER DE WORDE reached his destination next day, and both he and his book received a cordial reception from Fra Nicholas, who happened to be guest-master at the time and therefore was able to devote himself to the visitor.

The friar displayed almost as much satisfaction in Roger's book as its author himself. He turned the volume over tenderly in his hand. He was well acquainted with the gist of its contents and it was the desire of his heart to see the book multiplied and scattered broadcast over the land, for the holy man had reason to know that it contained a pearl of great price. A heavenly doctrine that would flare as a beacon light above the rocks and quicksands into which so many souls were heading, as even he himself had headed, once upon a time. The "showing" it contained would be for the salvation of numberless men of good-will, assailed by doubts in the present unrestful age.

Master de Worde and the friar sat late talking over the possibilities of the book which its owner had prudently replaced in his wallet lest impertinent eyes should fall on its contents before they had reached those of the prior who was to be interviewed on the following day. There was likely to be some little difficulty, Fra Nicholas warned his friend, as the prior was a man of cautious habit, as indeed need be in those times, and he might well hesitate in giving his permission for the multiplication of the work, failing some practical evidence of its usefulness as a direct antidote to the prevailing errors of the day. "If only the book could be shown to have actually effected the conversion of a Lollard, such concrete proof would place the matter beyond question."

"There is just such an one here at present," Fra Nicholas said. "A poor fellow who was once one of us but who hath lost his faith through dwelling on the evils of the times and forming his own conclusions, which hath warped his comprehension of the potency of the One who ruleth all things sweetly and well. He is full of scurrilous sayings against Holy Church, and sooner or later he must fall under the *Ex Officio* decree and suffer for his errors. At present he dwelleth near by in a place by himself and resisteth all that the prior can say to draw him from his error."

The face of Fra Nicholas grew sad as he spoke of the unfortunate brother. "If we could but get him to read thy book," he said to Master de Worde, "I verily believe that it might answer the questions that trouble him; for the message will come to him afresh in thy words, and he will take it with more gust as coming from a layman."

"Aye," Roger said eagerly, "and if so be that he did become converted from his error through its means, the prior would surely be convinced of its efficacy?"

"It seemeth that we have hit upon a great idea," the friar said. "Suppose we set about it at once. Fetch thy book and we will take it round and leave it with Thomas at his lodging and tell him that it is a new work by a lay clerk from Oxford." The friar gave a wry smile. "He will have hope to find some new heresy hidden therein," he said, "and that will move him to peruse it."

So it fell out that the pair of conspirators sought the lodging of Thomas the renegade, Roger bearing the precious work which he had retrieved from his wallet.

They knocked at the door of the unsanctified hermitage. Its inmate was a gaunt, hollow-cheeked man with a bitter smile, yet withal, with a hungry look in his eyes that provoked compassion. Fra Nicholas addressed him with full courtesy and explained their visit, as had been arranged. The ex-friar eyed the book with mild curiosity, and accepted it, with no great eagerness, it must be confessed. "My friend is fresh from Oxford," Fra Nicholas said, "and he is not without daring in the way he putteth the truth."

The Lollard brother brightened up a little at these words. "I will read the book if thou wish it," he observed, not too graciously. Young minds at Oxford might often be caught tripping, and heterodoxy was the meat and drink upon which the soul of ex-brother Thomas fed. To discover symptoms of "free thought" within the pale of the watchful Mother Church was the sole remaining joy of Thomas the renegade's poisoned and distempered existence. He smiled a sour smile, and retreated with the borrowed volume, promising that it should be returned duly.

They made their way back to the monastery, and Master de Worde retired to the guest-chamber and there prayed and kept vigil, importuning heaven that a miracle might happen and his book be shown to possess the power of converting a hardened heretic to the faith.

Fra Nicholas also prayed on his knees in his bare cell, using his scourge on his flesh, prayed that a lost sheep might be brought back to the fold. His thought and desire did not travel beyond the shepherd's point of view. He was a shepherd, first of all, and his desire was "held up" at the strayed sheep whose sin he was expiating on his own body.

It was not until the afternoon of the following day that Roger and Fra Nicholas were able to meet and pursue their conversation of the previous day. The former had delayed his introduction to the prior pending the result of the perusal of his book by the renegade brother. They had made a bold bid for a miracle, for little short of a miracle it would be if the soul-sick brother found healing in the pages of the revelation, inspired as it undoubtedly was.

They were pacing together in the long avenue leading to the monastery. Suddenly Fra Nicholas looked up. "Why," he cried, "I verily believe that yonder comes our friend himself." There was indeed a figure approaching in the distance, but Master de Worde presumed to contradict the assertion. "Nay," quoth he, "yonder fellow hath not the air of the man we saw last night, besides he cannot have read the book already."

"I hope he hath not repented of his promise to read it," the friar said. "It verily is Thomas, but thou art right, he doth not look the same." As the figure approached nearer it proved itself to be that of Thomas the renegade right enough, but an entirely new Thomas. Thomas the Lollard had a new face and a new manner of bearing himself. He advanced with alertness, but without any lack of that pleasing exterior quality which is called in religion modesty. He was smiling, but it was not the sinister smile of yesterday. In his hand he held Roger's volume.

Thomas the Lollard addressed himself to the clerk from Oxford. "Sir," he said, "I pray thee accept my most humble thanks. Thy book hath wrought a miracle in my soul."

Roger gasped. The friar crossed himself. "I know not what strange inspiration caused thee to bring it to me," the ex-brother went on.

"Verily it was the finger of God, for no man would have dreamed of such a resource, or kenned the way that it would work." He bent his head, and Fra Nicholas noted that he did so to hide the tears in his eyes. "There was never yet so wondrous a revelation of—of the ways of Divine Love." The speaker's voice lowered itself, and the tears conquered and rolled down his cheeks. He placed the book reverently in Roger's hands. Then he turned to Fra Nicholas. "I need absolution," he said, simply, and the friar laid his hand on his shoulder and led him away.

Master de Worde remained standing under the larches trying to realise the miracle that had taken place. He breathed his *Deo Gratias,* and then he glanced down at the book in his hand. He opened it, and he stared aghast. There met his eye a grotesque, elfish figure illuminated in red, blue and green. It was a picture of a ring of fairies dancing in a variety of wild attitudes, and it illustrated Sir Simon the parson's "booke of færie gestes."

The facts of the case were evident. He had gone to his wallet and abstracted the twin volume which had lain, forgotten and unheeded, beside the other, in place of the book of which he had been in search.

Master de Worde stood there gaping with perplexity. There could be no doubt as to the perfect sincerity of the man who had just returned him the book. There had been no bitter jest or mockery in that transfigured smile. Even now, as he looked up he could see him standing with the friar. The latter's hand was placed kindly on his shoulder as he stood with lowered head. It suggested penitence even more eloquently than if he had been on his knees. Roger durst not disturb them. He could only wait and wonder. He had not reckoned for a miracle of these dimensions.

A little later Fra Nicholas came over to where he stood. "Wait for me," he whispered, hurriedly, "I am taking him to the prior."

A few minutes afterwards he returned, and then Master de Worde heard what had happened.

Thomas the Lollard had taken the book and set himself down to read it at his table, trimming his lamp so that it might last the hours required. He had opened it and had been confronted, not by the learned exposition of a theologian, but by the representation of—it might have been Jack the giant-killer, or it might have been Hop o' my thumb. Naturally Thomas the Lollard was astonished. At first he, too, asked if it were a piece of mockery—an attempt to slay his doubts with ridicule. Then he bethought himself that it might be the devil gibing at the truths of religion by changing them into færie gestes. That was Thomas's second idea, færie gestes, in very sooth, these truths of which he had lost hold, and the loss of which had left his soul in blank misery. He had imbibed both as a child along with his mother's milk. As he sat thinking thus he began to read mechanically, and vagabond ideas began to seek a lodging through the open door of his mind. The truth and the færie gestes had both come from the same source. It was pleasing of God to let the children have the færie tales as well—a full homely thought of the Creator. Truth and færie tales. The truth was false, but the færie tales were true—God had made them to please the children. The devil didn't make the færie tales. So his mind worked on—the fragmentary portion of his brain not engaged in reading. He became very sleepy—his fantastic line of reasoning more involved.

"It was good of God to make the færie tales—God is good." Thomas the arch-doubter let his head drop forward. His forehead pressed on the gay page of the open book and he fell asleep. But his dreams were not of elves and goblins. As he slept there sounded in his ears the sweet note of a voice singing, as his mother used to sing when she was not reading him a færie geste. It was one of the hymns of the Church and he heard the words distinctly:— *Jesu, dulcis memoria*. It was not one of the hymns that his mother had used to sing, that was the curious part of it, but as he listened there came into his heart a strange new understanding of the love of which the hymn tells. He felt as though a block of ice were melting in his heart, and with the warmth there came a sudden light—a comprehension of the great doctrine of the all-abiding, the all-comprehending, the all-covering love of God, in Whom all good is grounded, so that all must and shall be well. "I It am that thou seekest! I It am that thou meanest! I It am that is the highest! I It am that is all!"

At this point in the narrative, Roger threw up his hands and grasped his head. "But that is in my book," he cried.

Fra Nicholas nodded. "'Tis a strange bewilderment," he said.

Then Roger remembered that he had yet to explain the presence of the twin-volume. He did so in as few words as possible.

Fra Nicholas was intensely interested. "'Tis strange," he remarked, "that one living in an anchorhold should have had the binding of the book for—I can tell thee this much without betrayal —'twas from an anchoress, a very holy and wonderful woman— that I heard the doctrine that lies within it. 'Twas she who received the revelation. Never since have I met such a soul, full of sweet enlightenment on heavenly things. I was minded of her," he went on, "when Thomas described to me the sweet singing in his dream for she used to sing to God in her solitude when she believed that none other were listening. I often caught her unawares. Her voice had a wonderful bird-like note that I have heard in none other."

Fra Nicholas's mind had wandered away into the past. "They brought me word that she was gone and that another occupied her anchorhold," he went on, "some poor unlettered soul like thou hast described."

"Well," Master Roger replied, sturdily, "mine at any rate had sufficient skill with her fingers, even though she were simple enough to hold my book and Sir Simon's færie gestes in equal esteem."

"Sir Simon?" Fra Nicholas echoed. "Where was it then that this anchoress of thine dwelt?"

Master Roger named the locality. Fra Nicholas opened his mouth to speak and closed it again. His expression of perplexity had deepened.

"'Tis a strange tangle," he said, "but the fact remaineth that God hath spoken to the heart of our friend. 'I It am that is all,'" he murmured softly, "'I It am that loveth tenderly and with all conde-scension. I It am that wrote of the færies for My little ones.'"

Master de Worde's disappointment anent his book being the instrument of brother Thomas's reconciliation was somewhat mitigated by the fact that the converted man gave his reason for regaining his faith in a manner that so remarkably coincided with those contained in Master de Worde's script that the prior was more than ready to allow a score or more of the brothers to set to in the Scriptorium and take down the book from dictation.

Other copies would be made from these, and so Master Roger's *opus magnum* would increase and multiply for the benefit of the heresy-ridden land at large. Moreover, Fra Nicholas was about to travel and might bear a copy with him to the Low Countries where he had been commissioned to preach, to counteract the wave of pseudo-mysticism which was sweeping the land as other forms of Lollardry were doing elsewhere. Fra Nicholas's absence would be an extended one, so Master de Worde had been just in the nick of time. So, taken on the whole it was in a satisfactory state of mind that Master Roger set out on his homeward journey.

When he reached the point where the road branched off to the left leading by way of the old abandoned highway to the chantry chapel on the cliff, Master de Worde hesitated. He intended to call upon Sir Simon in due course and to return his property, but he was also fain to climb the hill-side and say a kind word to the anchoress who had been at such pains to serve him. The good soul would be gratified to know that the book which she had had a hand in making (that was the way in which he would put it) was about to fulfil its destiny. Master Roger hitched his rein and rode onward along the desolate highway of other times. He dismounted at the churchyard gate that had once stood in the midst of the bustling caravans, but now in the solitude of the untrodden way. Very solitary the disused highway had become. The turning aside of the tide of teeming life had sequestrated it with a completeness that was almost eerie. There was an atmosphere of desolation about the forsaken mile. The old Cross Keys Inn stood in ruins. Its landlord had migrated to the village, to a newly built hostelry which bore the old name. It was late February and the birds were singing their mating song in the trees as Master de Worde climbed the path leading to the anchorhold. The sweet scent of violets was there, as of yore. They grew and flourished untended in the shadow of the ragged hedge. The birds and flowers, at any rate, were not oppressed by the subtle atmosphere of other days. But theirs was not the only joyous note. Suddenly there came, mingling with the song of the birds, the rich note of a woman's voice singing a melodious strain, softly, yet with a pure note of joy that was in curious harmony with the bridal song of the birds. It possessed, moreover, the same warbling quality so rare in the human voice—that natural gift which no skill in the teacher has been able to reproduce. Master Roger listened spell-bound. He could catch the words:—

> "Nec lingua valet dicere,
> Nec littera exprimere,
> Expertus potest credere,
> Quid sit Jesum diligere."

> But what to those who find? ah that
> Nor tongue nor pen can show
> The Love of Jesus what it is,
> None but His lov'd ones know.

It was the exact reproduction, to the very words of the hymn themselves, of the mystical dream-experience described by Fra Thomas. It also recalled to Roger, as in a flash, the description Fra Nicholas had given of the anchoress whom he had known, whose voice had the strange, bird-like note. What could it mean? Was he face to face once again with the supernatural? He glanced behind him. A small boy was standing there dangling a headless wooden horse in one hand and a horseless wooden head in the other.

"That be the mother singing," the small boy volunteered. "She do always sing as she works, and she do mostly sing that song."

Master de Worde thought a moment, then he put a question to his informant. "How long hath this same anchoress been up yonder?" he asked. "Hath there been always the same one there?"

The boy nodded. "Yes," he said, "'tis the same one. Some did say that she had gone and another come, but I know that she be the same, for God's Danny, the boatswain, told me so," the child wagged his head wisely, "and he knoweth, for Father Nicholas took him to the anchorhold at the same time when all the great people went there, and so he knows. Folk don't believe God's Danny because he's strange, but I do."

Master de Worde stood gazing abstractedly at the child. He was putting two and two together, and trying to realise the momentous four that it made. He remembered that the anchoress had told him that she had known Friar Nicholas a-many years ago; and Fra Nicholas had told him that he had once served Sir Simon the parson. Beyond doubt the present inmate of the anchorhold was no other than the holy and wonderful woman from whom Fra Nicholas had received the revelation of divine love duly set forth by Master de Worde in the book which the anchoress had been graciously permitted to bind!

The boy interrupted his cogitations.

"Be thou going to see the mother?" he asked.

"Yea, most certainly," Roger replied, yet with some hesitation.

The boy regarded him doubtfully. "Please, art thou in trouble?" he queried.

"N-no," Roger answered. "Why dost thou ask that?"

"Because," the boy explained, "the holy mother hath had the white cross put up on the tree, and that means that people 'of their charity, will not disturb her solitude unless they be in trouble.'"

"But thou art going to see her," Master Roger objected.

"Yea," was the reply, "but thou see, I *am* in trouble, I have broken off my horse's head."

Master Roger de Worde accepted the situation meekly. He made way for the other to pass and slowly wended his way down the path. He was fitting together the material in his head and trying to find the meaning. He sat himself down on a grave-mound and thought it out. The question remained, why should not his own book have possessed the same virtue as the other? The holy woman had sung her bridal song over both alike, to impregnate them with the virtue of her faith and sanctity, for that surely was the secret of Fra Thomas's mystical enlightening? Master de Worde's book, moreover, contained the very doctrine that was hers. It was in sooth her book, not his—Master Roger being, as has been stated at the beginning of this egregiously spun-out episode, a gentleman as well as a learned clerk, admitted this readily enough, albeit that it showed him what a coxcomb he had been in his conceit of himself. Why had the book of færie gestes been chosen rather as the vehicle for the miracle of grace?

And then it was that, seated outside the anchorhold on the mound that covered the dust of some poor fisher-body, Master Roger de Worde received a "showing" that was verily all his own, for there and then, it was borne in upon his ghostly understanding that all the intellectual treasure that lay stored in the volume written by himself and conceived by the other, possessed in God's sight no tittle more value than a book of færie gestes as compared with an act of perfect humility, for the things by which miracles are wrought are humility and the sweet love of God in the heart. So Roger de Worde carried his showing home to Oxford full deep down in his heart; and when, many years later, he produced the book which was his own in very sooth, it was but a ghostly discourse on the blissful virtue of humility. And of this book his great-grandson Wynkyn, about half a century later made many copies on his new and wonderful press for the imprinting of books.

Chapter XX

His Majesty's Jongleur

RIAR NICHOLAS sat amongst the sand dunes on the seashore gazing on the waters which divided him from his native soil. He was making a meditation on the land of his birth, to which he was shortly to return after an exile of some years. He had been preaching in the cities of the Low Countries where a subtle form of heresy was being promulgated by a sect of so-called mystics. The reason of his being sent was that Friar Nicholas himself possessed a message, mystical, yet withal quite simple and approved to the full by Holy Church. A wondrous message of Love and well-being, divinely calculated to win those souls for whom the devil had laid snares in the shape of "comfortable sayings" in regard to the shriving of sins and works of penance, "spiritual priesthood," and the like. Never had the unchangeable message of the Church been conveyed with such sweetness and speedfulness as in the form in which Friar Nicholas delivered it to men of good will distraught by the errors and confusions of the times.

Friar Nicholas meditated in the Ignatian fashion, quite fortuitously, of course. He made his composition of place. It was an anchorhold built up against a church. Of its inmate he could but make a picture which had always been one of the imagination, for he had never set eyes on the Anchoress to whom he had given housling and with whom he had conversed during that period of his career when his soul had suffered from growing pains. He called to

memory, however, her voice, and the words that she had spoken—
that strange and wondrous, yet so simple, revelation of divine love
that had moved the world to trust in the ultimate wellness of all.
Its truths were so deep, and withal so tender. They had cast a light
on the mystery of sin which was indeed the light of Faith, leading
one to the blissful human Friend and Lover, full friendly and courteous in his words with the sinner. He contemplated the marvel of
it all. That this tender message should have come through one who
had embraced the most repellently austere form of life—the life
against which these new preachers inveighed with all the scorn at
their command. The sweet, heartening message of clemency had
come to her within her four walls—the four walls which were love,
and in the centre of which, safe from intrusion, there dwelt Love.

These men amongst whom he moved with his message had
talked of the "falsehood of imprisoning walls"—nay, had he not
thought thus himself at one time?—and between encompassing
walls she had found the infinite. Infinite pity, infinite understanding, infinite love.

He continued his composition of place, and pictured the two
little windows to the cell. The one through which she received
God, and the one through which she gave Him to others. It was
the great outstanding danger that assailed those who dwelt recluse
to prefer this latter window, but how ferociously she had combated
that menace. He thought of the white cross on the tree. And then
he thought of the story told him by "God's Danny," and that Easter
Morning when she told him that she had a message for him to pass
on to the world. Yea, verily it was the narrowing walls that had
enabled her to see all humanity in a point—in one figure—that
hanging on the Cross; and in that figure all humanity.

And now she was with the saints. Another dwelt in her anchorhold—so they declared. Sometimes he wondered if they had
spoken truly. There had been no means of finding out. That had
been a strange thing that Roger de Worde had told him anent her

successor. As his meditation branched off in this speculative direction there came a sound of someone approaching. It was a queer vagabond fellow, a minstrel, evidently, for he was clad in weather-stained, fantastic garb, and carried his instrument on his back. He wore odd leggings, the motley of the professional entertainer, and the hood which was drawn over his head gave a grotesque conventual twist to his appearance.

The stranger saluted the friar respectfully in his native tongue, and right glad Nicholas was to hear it again. Finding themselves to be compatriots they fell into conversation—a discussion of the weather and the prospects of a smooth voyage next day when, the jongleur told the friar, he was hoping to return home in one of the fishing smacks lying in the harbour. The priest informed his companion that he, too was returning to England shortly.

"Then it were no good," the jongleur said, "for me to offer my humble services to bear a message to anyone for Thy Reverence."

The friar considered the offer. "Thou wilt not be in the whereabouts of the port in about a week from thy landing, I suppose," he said, "if that had been the case I might have taken thee at thy word and begged thee to find out for me if by any chance the anchorhold under the beacon tower of St. Catherine be still occupied by the anchoress who was there a-many years ago. 'Twas when I was chantry priest there," he went on, "before I joined the friars, that the anchorhold was occupied by a marvellous woman that called herself Mother Catherine. She taught me many things, and did me such good service for my soul's weal as I could never tell any man. They brought me tidings that she had gone and another had taken her place—one vastly different in every way." He sighed and gazed out over the ocean.

The jongleur shot a swift glance at the speaker. This man with the celestial countenance, marked with the lines of a rigid asceticism, was treating him as he might have treated a fellow-churchman rather than as one who all but came under the ban of the Church.

"I, too, knew the Mother Catherine who was there a-many years ago," he said. "Verily a marvellous woman for she slew the Lady Editha de Beauville." He glanced at the other and saw that his quip needed elucidating. "I knew the holy mother out in the world," he explained, "when she was the Lady Editha, heiress of the de Beauville wealth. The Lady Editha entered the anchorhold, and in a few years' time there was no Lady Editha left, but one Dame Catherine, a passing holy lady that had no traffic with any save in spiritual matters, and was fiercely detached from the things that were the breath of the nostrils of the Lady Editha."

The friar had become visibly interested. "The holy anchoress never spoke to me of her life in the world," he said. "What thou sayest is of no small interest to me. I pray thee tell me more. 'Tis no idle curiosity on my part."

"Nay, forsooth," the other replied, "for to know the saint in his full stature thou must know his old Adam. That which made the Dame Catherine whom I knew so mighty interesting, 'twas surely her old Adam."

"Good friend," the friar said, later on, as struck by a thought. "If thou could'st find out for me if the holy mother be indeed gone to her reward, as they do declare, and if so be, the place of her burial, I would gladly make a pilgrimage thither to pay respect to her memory, but I have no taste to interview this successor of hers, God forgive me. I can hardly believe it possible that there could have been so strange a mistake. If indeed it were so she would have felt herself shamefully deserted by one who owed her everything."

"I will take on thy commission right readily," the jongleur said, "and thou wilt find me on thy landing awaiting thee with the information thou requirest. God grant that it may be good hearing for thee, reverend father." He became silent for the space it might be of a *Veni Creator*. Then he spoke again, interrupting the other's thoughts, which were running on what the stranger had told him concerning the fascinating Lady Editha de Beauville, the holy mother anchoress's "old Adam." Verily the picture of the saint had received its true colouring. This strange fellow was right—extraordinarily right!

"I will tell thee now something about this Mother Catherine who now occupies the anchorhold," the jongleur said. "'Tis said of her that she be a penitent that is expiating a sinful past. Moreover, they say that, there in her cell, she hath warped towards Lollardry and done mischief to those that came to visit her. The nuns that have the care of her, so 'tis said, are in very terror of holding ghostly converse with her lest she contaminate their faith. In good sooth, if it could be that it was the self-same holy lady of a-many years ago, the voice of slander hath been busy at work and changed her into a woman of no repute."

The listener sprang to his feet. "Impossible!" he shouted—he had almost got back to young Sir Nicholas, the chantry priest, in the vigour of his protest. "Could envy and malice indeed have done this whilst she sat a prisoner between four walls—stripped her of all was hers, and clad her in vile rags and a crown of thorns?"

"How now, how now, holy father," the jongleur said, calmly. He had swung his instrument over his shoulder and was running his fingers over the strings. "Thou art surely mistaken in saying that she was enclosed all the time within four walls. For did not God lead her out into the land of Vision (if so be that this thing happened to her) and there bid her offer her Isaac—her first-born whom she loved. And upon a hill which He showed her, not, mark ye, one of her choosing. And there He bade her offer her sacrifice in a place which is called 'the Lord seeth.' Perchance, holy father, she had to leave thee behind with the young men and the ass?"

The friar sat regarding his companion in wonderment. What manner of man was this?

"Who art thou?" he cried, impulsively, "who doth preach the secrets of God in such strange guise."

"My name is Fiddlemee," the other replied, "and I am known as the King's jongleur."

"Tell me thy history," the friar said, looking into the quaint, seamed countenance, with its queer, expressive mouth and glistening eyes. The other proceeded to do so, quite simply. "A-many years ago, when I was a youth," he said, "I did of my impudence think to enter religion and become a monk. They took me as a novice at a certain monastery of good repute, and I had liking enough for the life—so much so that I was for ever laughing and making mad sport amongst the brothers, and it pleased not my lord abbot, this lightness in me. Well, one day evil befell the house. There was sickness and lean living, and ill-repute snapping at our heels, and the brethren grew glum-faced and heavy; and so to make good cheer I fashioned myself an instrument of a sort, and sung them a ribald song of the world,—for, myself, I was yet full of mirth and felt as much liking as ever of the life, since the Lord had willed all that came to pass. And the brethren indeed grew cheerful, but my lord abbot took great scandal at my levity, and he called me to the parlour and he said to me, 'I will have no more of thee. Thy vocation is to sing light songs to a light world. Go thou and do it, for thou art a light fellow.' And since that I was yet at that moment under obedience to him as my superior, for all that after the words were spoken it came to an end, I straightly and strictly did that which he bade me, and I went forth and sang light songs to a light world; and I be doing so still, and so shall I as long as there be those willing to listen, for so, methinks, it was the will of God that spoke through my superior. And so it be," he ended, "like the light fellow that I am, I call myself the King's jongleur."

The friar regarded him with eyes in which the tears were standing. He stretched out his hand. "Brother," he said, "thy task is a hard one and thou hast faced the heat of the day. Thou hast earned thy rest. Come and spend thy playtime at our House of

Blackfriars, whither I go to be prior. I promise thee I will not hold thee a light fellow."

The jongleur gazed wistfully before him over the sea. "I thank Thy Reverence," he said, "and when my working day is over most gladly will I accept thy offer of asylum. When I grow to croak my song like a frog in a marsh so that men take to casting mud at me, then I will avail myself of thy charity, and that right readily."

"Well," the prior-elect said, smiling, "I hold thee to this compact—nay, methinks I will hold myself as already thy superior and claim thee under holy obedience."

The other looked at him whimsically. "Thy Reverence hath not as yet had a sample of my wares," he observed. He placed Orpheus on his faded red knee and struck a chord. "We have been speaking of anchorholds," he said, "I will sing Thy Reverence a song of an anchorhold—a riddle, for riddling is my trade."

The other disposed himself to listen, and Fiddlemee began:—

> "Be mine a holy anchorhold,
> A solitude of two.
> No vain disturbance making bold
> Shall creep my window through.
> Yet many a sight and many a sound,
> Yea all I love shall yet be found
> Within my fastness true,
> So but I make my anchorhold
> A solitude of two.
>
> Within my holy anchorhold—
> My solitude of two—
> Dwell all my kith and all my kind,
> For all God's heart can hold I find
> Within my fastness true,
> So be it in my anchorhold
> He hath His dwelling too.

The Anchorhold

For He hath bared His heart and shown
Therein my riddle's clue.
There dwelleth all I hold my own
As in a fastness true.
Aye, all my loves, or great or small,
He shows me whilst I dwell, withal,
Within a holy anchorhold,
A solitude of two."

At its finish the listener stretched out his hand for a second time. Fiddlemee dropped on to his stiff knees and kissed it. And so he knelt there and received his blessing. At last the King's jongleur had come into his own.

Chapter XXI

There Came a Knight a-Riding

MASTER HUBERT, the taverner, was entertaining a distinguished guest at the new Cross Keys Inn, opposite the church on the King's highway, which no longer diverted from its straight course on the way to the second city in England. Master Hubert's guest was a magnificent person, a knight to wit, wearing the insignia of the crusaders on his cloak. He was a man of middle age. Fair, with a fine countenance and upright bearing, with a bronzed cheek that accentuated the fairness of his golden hair, and the brightness of his frank blue eyes. Sir Aleric de Burgh's boyhood was well preserved in the matured citizen of the world, nor had his eyes ceased to be a place of dreams and visions. It was an extraordinarily comely countenance, taken from the viewpoint of the angels as well as that of Master Hubert, who found his guest a fine figure of an Englishman.

The knight rode unattended, and had made his business known to his host immediately on his arrival. Sir Aleric de Burgh wished to visit the holy woman living in the anchorhold. He had brought her a relic from the holy places which he was fain to deliver over to her.

It was many a year since Hubert the taverner had entertained a distinguished visitor bound on a like errand. He informed the newcomer with some bluntness that such was the case. The anchoress was no longer the vogue. The changing of the course of the high road had partly accounted for this; but in addition to that, the anchoress had fallen into bad repute. Some said that she had made free with the Lollards, others that much worldly commerce had turned her head. At any rate nobody in these days dreamt of diverting the course of his journey in order to call at the anchorhold. The villagers went up there sometimes to get the anchoress to pray for their sick cattle, or to mend their broken chattels with the fish glue that she got from the fisher-folk.

The visitor listened with a flushed cheek and kindling eye. Mine host was seized with discretion and suppressed a hint as to the doubts cast upon the enclosed lady's past reputation. The stalwart knight was fingering the hilt of his sword, as it was, in a suggestive manner.

The visitor took his refreshment in a great hurry. He left his steed at the inn and started to make the pilgrimage on foot. It was a delicate and chivalrous tribute to the holy mother whose reputation had been so vulgarly impugned. Twenty years had not obliterated the image of the lady of the tourney from his heart. He had been in love then. He remained in love now. He had gone into the battle of the cross breathing her name after that of our Blessed Lady herself, and the memory of the eager, glowing face, with its strange mixture of the child and the seer—of impulse and calm vision—had never faded or lost its stimulating properties. He pictured her leading the extraordinary life into which her indomitable spirit had thrust her. He thought of the frail sheath which held that two-edged blade and wondered how it had fared during these years of merciless austerities.

He would not be able to see to judge for himself, but he would hear her voice, now that he had earned his right to visit her—that wonderful voice of hers. And he could tell her that he had battled for the cross and the holy places, a true knight and faithful to his inspiration.

It was summer and the flowers were in full bloom. In the path to the lonely anchorhold, however, there was left blooming but one rose, and a single lily waving on its tall stem. Sir Aleric could not but compare it with his last visit, the day of the enclosing, when the precincts of the anchorhold had been laid out and bedded like the bower of a queen. He rang the little bell and stole softly up to the window. The fine chivalry of his nature gathering up all the worship and veneration of his heart to make, as it were, a great amend. He heard the sound of movement within, and his heart stood still, as the heart of the other lover, Godiva, had stood still on her day.

"*Dominus tecum*," said the well-remembered voice. The tone was interrogative.

Sir Aleric pressed his head against the stone mullion. "*Et cum spiritu tuo*," he answered, hastily.

"Who speaketh to me?" the recluse asked. There was a faint tone of apprehension.

"Aleric de Burgh," he answered. "I am just returned from the Holy Land and I have brought thee a flower from the Garden of Gethsemane." He produced a tiny packet from his scrip and pushed it with a trembling hand through the window, up against the folds of the curtain.

The latter was lifted half an inch and the packet disappeared beneath it, but not so much as a finger of the anchoress's hand was exposed to view.

"I thank thee for so precious a gift," the anchoress said, but her tone was cold and distant. The very jealous knight, Sir Chastity, had placed himself beside the little window with his sword of flame.

Cold as its tones were the voice thrilled the listener. It conjured up the vision of the past as vividly as sight itself. He could find no words to come to his aid. Silence is a sad tale-bearer.

"And hast thou battled for the Cross all these years?" the anchoress enquired when she had made the silence marked enough on her side to be discouraging.

"All these last five years," Sir Aleric replied. "I durst not come to thee before, for thou didst forbid that I came save that I brought thee a message from the holy places."

"Then is this holy relic but an excuse for thy visit?" the anchoress asked, icily. She had become wonderfully like the long-dead Lady Editha. The tones recalled vividly to the listener the imperious prohibition. The Lady Editha, with her eyes shooting out light and her head poised exquisitely, had stood answering his meek pleading.

"But I may come when thou art enclosed and speak with thee at thy window?"

"Thou mayst come when thou hast been through the Holy Wars, and hast a message from the holy places, not otherwise. Those who would visit me must *keep to the point*."

Had he received his answer in the manner of the woman who had "some cunning with the glue-pot," who prayed efficaciously for sick cows, and was ever intensely interested in the subjects under discussion, the past might indeed have become a dream to Sir Aleric de Burgh—dead and beyond recall, but the very zealous knight Sir Chastity had allowed his valour to outrun his discretion—or shall we say, his strategic faculty. There remained in the anchoress a spark of the long-dead spirit of the Lady Editha de Beauville that was in danger of being fanned into life by this sound of a voice that carried in its tone that reverential love that had been the daily portion of the solitary, as well as of the great lady, in the old days when the pilgrims came that way to learn ghostly wisdom from the woman who had given up all. Sir Chastity raised his sword to smite, and in the doing of it, if one may dare say so, over-reached himself, for the humble mother anchoress made answer in the tones of the long-dead Lady Editha, and Sir Aleric, kneeling at her curtained window felt his heart thrill at the living vision of the past.

"Holy mother thou art hard on me," he said, his voice vibrant with the emotion of the moment. "Hast thou no kinder word for me than this? I have indeed been through the Holy Wars, and I have carried ever before me to strengthen my lance, the undying memory of that day after the tourney, when thou didst sit as a queen at the banquet telling of thy choice of this great renouncement. That vision hath never left me——" He was interrupted.

"Thou shalt carry a new vision—one that shall drive out this other, in good sooth," responded the voice of the Lady Editha de Beauville, for the long-dead lady seemed to have sprung back into life. Like the upshooting flame of an expiring candle her personality was flaring out for the last time. "My rule," it went on, "doth permit me to withdraw my curtain if the necessity be direful, and never, methinks, was a more direful necessity than now." The curtain was withdrawn with characteristic swiftness. The lady within was acting on impulse—applying a drastic measure to meet the occasion. The Lady Editha de Beauville had in verity got back and was making the most of her time. "Look thee well and see the vanity that thou hast placed foremost in thy thought—thou, a knight of Our Lady!"

The cure was indeed drastic but it should be efficacious. Sir Aleric found himself gazing on a face instead of on the concealing curtain. The worn, desolated countenance of a woman who had remorselessly trampled upon nature for twenty years—slain all comeliness with the high hand of unremitting hardship. Hollow-cheeked, scanty-locked, with all the natural accessories of beauty missing or thinned out. Wasted by sickness. With this abiding vision the Lady Editha de Beauville would exorcise that other which he had worn on his heart throughout the high adventure.

She looked him in the eyes, calmly and steadily, and with strange, exultant triumph, but only for a couple of seconds, then the curtain was drawn again with even greater swiftness. This time it was the swiftness of fear, for the faded eyes of the anchoress had met those of her true knight, and in the latter they had read something that was unexpected—terrifying.

Sir Aleric bent his head before the dividing curtain in a transport of worship.

It is not given to the eye of man to look upon uncreated beauty, but Sir Aleric had caught the vision as it had ever been, a shaft of God's glory glinting on a little clay, and the intervening years had possessed another than a diminishing property.

So he knelt on in his transport; and the very holy knight, Sir Chastity, dropped upon his knee and worshipped likewise.

.   .   .   .   .

Meanwhile there was silence in the anchorhold. The visitor had been dismissed. Perhaps an hour after his departing footsteps had echoed on the path the curtain was withdrawn. The anchoress peeped through and saw lying on the ledge another floral offering—a lily and a rose, fresh gathered from her garden. Hastily she drew the curtain again. The holy anchoress was deeply troubled in mind on a point of conscience. When her attendants arrived she meekly implored them to place the cross on the tree that she might have quiet to think over her sins, and if so be, could they send her father confessor to her aid.

But the anchoress's father confessor was lying ill and bedridden. He was all but a centenarian in years. Day after day she waited, but he came not, and on the ninth day she made a prayer to Heaven that some ghostly sign might be given to set her mind at rest, for it was no light thing that she, a holy incluse, had done in the inexplicable impulse of the moment. Then she rose from her knees and crossed over and withdrew her curtain and looked out at God's world again; and lo! on the ledge there lay the lily and the rose as fresh as though they had been that moment plucked. And the recluse lady put out her hand and drew them in and laid them beside the dried flower from the Garden of Gethsemane, for she knew it to be the true answer to her prayer, showing her that it was indeed sweet St. Chastity who had withdrawn her curtain for her and given the new vision to the pure and faithful eyes of her true knight.

Chapter XXII

Merrily End, Magnificat!

IDDLEMEE WAS in the wars—or rather Orpheus his lute was. Fiddlemee had met a caitiff, or was it a varlet?—on the road who had disapproved of his music and had lifted his foot against Orpheus, as venerable as his white-haired master. The body of the lute showed a long, ugly crack which required to be treated with good strong fish glue, lest the rift should render Orpheus's music mute.

There had been no Flipkin to render dental justice to the caitiff, for Flipkin had succumbed to a good old age many years ago and his master walked alone along the high road that had once upon a time passed beneath the beacon chapel of St. Catherine. No one lighted the beacon in these days Fiddlemee had been told. The men whose business it was to look after it had shied at the task because, they declared, the anchoress who lived up against the chapel was a witch and they feared to approach after dark. Fiddlemee heard all this from Master Hubert at the Cross Keys Inn in the new highway where he stopped for refreshment. The mention of the anchoress, coupled with the sight of the sad condition of Orpheus, had suggested an idea to the sympathetic Hubert. The anchoress did a bit of mending and possessed some good strong fish glue which she might lend to Fiddlemee for the patching up of his instrument. Some said that she had been sick, but she would be well enough now to see to that much.

Fiddlemee accepted the suggestion with alacrity. Master Hubert was a mighty resourceful fellow, deserving of a song all to himself. He slapped his stiff, rheumatic thigh and essayed a skip in the air. The anchoress's glue pot would solve the whole difficulty. He would go and beg the loan of it from her at once. "Moreover," quoth he, "I have a question to ask of the good mother so all arranges itself well. I hereby remove the murrain from the varlet whose boot disapproved of my love-ditty.

"'Twas on the boot, not on the man, that I called down a plague," Fiddlemee explained, "for the soul of a man is immortal whereas that of a boot is not."

"Get thee out," mine host said, "and play not so with thy words to the mother anchoress or she will not lend thee her glue pot."

Fiddlemee, his repast finished, possessed himself of his wounded instrument and started forth on his quest. He was in magnificent form, albeit that he went slowly up the hill, stopping ever and anon to get breath. Now and again he gave vent to his feelings by slapping a thigh, now a blue one, now a red one, for he wore his customary fantastic garb.

When he reached the anchoress's pathway he cast swift, observant glances to right and left. He stood for a moment gazing down on the forgotten road, grass-grown and neglected. He could see the distant line of the new straight road. He fondled Orpheus and struck a thin, unvibrant note that somehow seemed to suit the occasion. Then he marked the ragged borders of the flower bed. Wild flowers and weeds were there in profusion. The kind of flowers that grow in cottage gardens.

Fiddlemee crossed over to the little window. He remembered it well on the occasion of his visit as his Grace the Duke's emissary. That had been a curiously similar errand to this, for of course the loan of the glue-pot was a secondary matter. The Duke had bade him assure himself that it was really the Lady Editha de Beauville; and now he was here in order to assure another that it was really the holy Mother Catherine and not a poor penitent of no repute.

Fiddlemee was quoting something to himself. "The Kingdom of Heaven is like unto a treasure hidden in a field." And again:— "If a man shall have given all the substance of his house for love he shall despise it as nothing."

But first he had to find out.

He sat down and tapped hard with his knuckles on the ledge.

"Good mother," he shouted. "Good mother, I want the loan of thy glue pot!"

"Who art thou?" came the answer. "Hast thou something for me to mend?"

"I be a wandering minstrel that hath had his lute kicked into holes by a varlet on the highway," Fiddlemee replied. "He liked not my song."

"Was it an evil song?" the voice enquired, quickly.

"Nay, mother," Fiddlemee responded, "'twas the lack of evil that he kicked at. 'Twill not befoul the hairs of thy brush to dress the wounds of my poor old Orpheus."

"I fear the window were too narrow for thee to pass me in the lute," the anchoress said, "or I would gladly heal his wounds myself. I am told that I have great cunning with the glue brush. But wait a moment and I will give thee the glue pot." A minute later a large and very sticky pot was thrust through the window. Fiddlemee caught sight of at least three of the anchoress's fingers and crossed himself.

He took the pot and applied his nose to it cautiously, with an anticipatory grimace. Fish-glue is evil-smelling stuff, as a rule. He sniffed again. "Good mother," he said, "thy fish-glue smelleth like a potion of rose-leaves. Thou hast disguised it cunningly—nay, but it is rather violets and lilies of the valley." He proceeded to smear a brushful of the glue over the crack, and as he did so he continued to converse genially with the inmate of the anchorage. His tones were friendly rather than deferential.

"Ah, well," he commented, harking back to Orpheus's misadventure, "all that one meets on the road, Grammacy, be not varlets.

I met me earlier, for the nonce, a beautiful knight that had turned palmer and was on his way back to Holy Land because that since that he had returned from fighting he had seen a vision, which same did make him wishful to do real things rather than play games in much fine harness and with good living and all the honours of war. A most beautiful knight it was, by name Sir Aleric de Burgh."

There was a comment from within. "God be with him," said the anchoress.

"But, to speak of holy people," Fiddlemee went on, "when I was over in Flanders a se'nnight since, it might be, I did happen to meet there a holy friar, one Nicholas, who prayed me discover for him where the anchoress who was here before thee lies buried. A very holy woman she was, so they say (he winked across at a nodding daisy) though I doubt me not, without thy cunning with the glue-pot. There was a story about that did recently reach his ears that she had never died at all. He bade me make sure, or else find out where they had buried her, as he would fain pay respect to her relics, for she was a very holy woman"—Fiddlemee slightly accentuated the *she*—"albeit that she had no skill with the glue-pot."

He paused and scraped a lump of glue off his finger-nail.

"Hast thou dressed the wound of Orpheus to thy satisfaction?" the inmate of the anchorage asked.

"Perfectly, thanks to thy medicine, holy mother chirurgeon," Fiddlemee replied. "But I have in sooth promised to find out for the good father where the holy lady lies buried and I pray thee help me in this matter."

He received an answer this time. "Is it not usual to bury a holy anchoress in her anchorhold? The holy mother anchoress of whom thou speakest lies buried here. Tell the good friar so, and tell him that it would be scant courtesy on his part to visit the cell of a living woman in order to pay reverence to the dead."

Fiddlemee sat there listening to the answer. He set Orpheus aslant on his knee and his fingers crept round the long thin neck of the instrument. He touched the strings lightly with his other hand. He had taken much the same message many years ago to another would-be visitor, but although similar in purport, the distance of the poles lay between the two. "If a man hath given all the substance of his house for love he shall despise it as nothing." Nay, would he take a particle of it back, were it so offered? "Love is as strong as death. Jealousy is as hard as hell. What to nature is as death and the pains of hell shall not be stronger than love."

The voice that sent the message today was natural and very gentle. The latter part of the message, moreover, contained that touch of humour that sounded a harmonic note in the jongleur's soul. His eyes sparkled with a kind of radiant mirth. He struck a ringing chord on the lute. The tone of Orpheus had regained its pristine vigour. It was like a rich and sounding note of victory—of final triumph.

Then he set the instrument aside and picking up the glue-pot placed it on the ledge where Sir Aleric had laid his posy. He knelt down, as the other had done. "Holy mother," he said, and his tones had become those of the devout pilgrim, known to the holy anchoress of yore, "I return thee thy pot-pourri of roses and violets. Orpheus will for ever sing with sweeter tone in that he hath had his hurts dressed from it. Pray for his master that he may make sweet music for his *Nunc Dimittis*."

"Who art thou? I seem to know thy voice."

The question came in quick tones of anxious enquiry.

"I am Fiddlemee that once had a dog called Flipkin," came the reply. "I was in the service of my lord the baron who gave the great tourney whereat were wrought deeds braver than Agincourt. At which the Lady Editha de Beauville was named queen of beauty just before she purchased the field where lay hidden a treasure. 'Twas she that inhabited this anchorhold, until thy predecessor, the very holy 'Dame Catherine' did slay her, even as thou hast slain the very holy Mother Catherine that lies buried in thy cell."

He paused and waited the reply. It came:

"But thou hast not heard the ending of the story. How His Reverence the King's chaplain, as he lay sick, did send a letter to the anchoress making confession that it was not he who made the discourse——"

"Sshh!" She was interrupted; and a loud, warning chord from Orpheus brought her to a pause. "Stay, stay, holy mother," Fiddle-mee cried, "methinks in sooth the good chaplain hath been punished for his heresy in making confession to a woman in that she hath broken the seal and seeketh to tell another the secret. But, for the credit of thy sex, holy mother, pass it on no further."

There was an answering sound within. A little ripple of silver laughter, low, and no longer full and rounded, but still containing the music of laughing water. Fiddlemee's head was thrown backward. His laugh was the *risus dentium* permissible only in lay folk. He was enjoying the merriest jest of his life, and they laughed together in harmony, and the mirth of the onlooking angels was doubtless joined to theirs for it was a fit and merry ending to the story of the treasure hidden in a field.

"Orpheus oweth thee a song," Fiddlemee cried, "in return for thy charity." He rose to his feet and struck a chord on the lute, and burst forth into song:—

"Magnificat anima mea Dominum: et exsultavit spiritus meus in Deo salutari meo."

Chapter XXIII

The Beacon

HE ONLY CONSOLATION left to the crew of the *Stella Maris* was that they had a holy man on board whose prayers might even yet avail to save them from their parlous plight. The night was pitchy black and they were in all probability drifting towards the quicksands. Their captain had completely lost his bearings owing to a mishap to Master Boatswain's magnetic needle which, afloat on a piece of wood in a pan of water, was an unfailing guide to the mariner. The boatswain, a strange religious fellow called "God's Danny," was praying his hardest to make up for the lack of his tool; and all the crew, fishermen out on their business on the high seas, were good Catholics who heard their Jesu Mass at the chantry chapel when on shore. The passenger, who had elected this rough method of making the journey home from Flanders, was a holy friar preacher; the fame of whose sanctity had gone abroad. In his prayers the hope of the crew rested at this dark moment of suspense. He, for his part, was praying with all his might and main, not merely that his own life might be spared and those of the crew, but that he might not be prevented from fulfilling a mission that awaited him over on that other shore. A great wrong was waiting there to be righted. A fair name which had been befouled by malice and slander and misunderstanding had to be cleared of its shame. Fra Nicholas's vague doubts as to the truth of the story of the anchoress's death which he had expressed to the jongleur had been proved since to have been well founded. On the sea-shore, attached to the fishing smack from England, the *Stella Maris*, Fra Nicholas had come across God's Danny, whom as a lad he had befriended after hearing the strange story which had made "God's Danny" out of the erstwhile "No-man's Danny." To the delighted Danny, after due enquiries as to his own history and well-being, he had repeated his question concerning the identity of the inmate of the anchorage. Danny had set the matter beyond doubt. It was most truly the same Mother Catherine of old days, but since the new road had been made no more pilgrims had come that way, people said queer things about the holy mother now-a-days. Some that she once had been no better than she ought to be, others that she was affected to dangerous heresies. Others, again, that she was a poor simple soul who had taken the place of the former inmate when she had tired of her life, and wished to withdraw privily so that the voice of gossip might be silenced. Most people stuck to it that there had been two Dame Catherines.

Fra Nicholas had listened in burning indignation. He remembered among other things, his friend Roger de Worde's story of the anchoress who had been graciously permitted to bind the book which contained the revelation. And he recalled the subsequent mysterious happenings, and the divine comedy of the færie gestes. She had ever been greedy to give all—but she had needed to be taught what that all meant. How truly the "light" brother in the motley habit had put it. She had indeed been led into a land, and to a mountain "that had been shown to her." And she had offered there her Isaac—her very identity! And, truly, truly, she had left her companions behind so that the place might in sooth be called "the Lord God sees."

He knelt there in the boat drifting to destruction and prayed with all his strength that he might be allowed to live to vindicate her—to restore her Isaac and substitute the ram.

Suddenly as he prayed, with his head buried in his hands, there was a shout. "The beacon! The beacon! They have lighted the beacon! We are heading for the quicksands. Heave her round."

Sure enough, in the distance in front of them there had shot up a flame of light. It could be nothing else than the beacon on the chapel of St. Catherine, up on the home cliff. "Head her round! Head her round, we are on the sands," the first speaker repeated, and with all hands at work the boat veered round and altered her course. The canvas was adjusted and she moved away from danger in the direction where a safe landing could be effected. There was no longer need to hesitate in choosing their course. The peril was over. The crew of the *Stella Maris* was safe.

The dawn was reddening in the sky when they finally brought the *Stella Maris* to shore. It was in the little cove above which the guiding light had blazed from the spot where the chantry chapel stood.

Much-needed rest and refreshment awaited the famished crew in the cottages of the fisher folk which clustered on the beach under the shadow of the cliff, but their distinguished passenger was firm in declining the hospitality pressed upon him by the grateful mariners, who frankly attributed their deliverance to his prayers. He was anxious to make his thanksgiving in his own priestly way, and he reckoned that if he reached the chapel before the priest left after saying Mass the latter might permit him to say his own Mass of thanksgiving. The holy lady in the anchorhold would vouch for his *bona fides*, if necessary.

The boatswain, "God's Danny," insisted on accompanying him to serve his Mass. They climbed the path up the cliff. The way was familiar. How strange that chance should have cast him up on this very spot instead of miles away at the sea-port for which they had been bound. It surely meant that his mission of restitution was a sacred one. It might have been yesterday that he had hastened up that very path to interview the holy mother anchoress on the absorbing subject of his soul, and (let us be fair to even our young selves) the souls of others. He was tired out and famished, yet there was a kind of buoyancy of spirit which kept him up. He felt strangely like young Sir Nicholas, the dreamer. The sense of home-coming was in itself exhilarating in spite of the holy indifference which a half a score of years in religion had taught him. He thought of the altar in the sanctuary which he was approaching. His first altar, where he had said Our Lady's Mass daily, and from whence he had given her weekly housling to the holy inmate of the adjacent anchorhold. She would be behind the little narrow, deep-cut window in the chancel when he said his Mass, looking upon the uplifted Host. It was almost impossible to realise.

The winding path had brought them to the brow of the cliff and now the chapel came in sight. How difficult it was to realise that he had ever been away. Approaching from the direction of the convent he saw a young priest. His companion informed him that it was the chantry priest on his way to say Mass.

The young man was evidently in a hurry, and perturbed about something. Nicholas hesitated to address him, but he himself paused and regarded the other questioningly.

Fra Nicholas introduced himself, and without wasting words over the events of the night made his request straight away.

"If thou wouldst wish it thou couldst say thy Mass now," the chaplain answered, "in place of mine, for I am sorely put about seeing to one that lies sick, and I would be in sooth thankful for thy aid." He seemed thoroughly flustered, and almost beside himself. He was a very young man. Fra Nicholas felt sorry for him. "Trouble no more," he said, practically, "but get thee on thy way. I have here my server, and I will say Mass for the good folk, as I have done many a time before."

The other thanked him in a rather bewildered way and glanced backward towards the convent. "'Tis the anchoress that hath been taken ill," he explained, "and I am waiting for the sisters that look after her to come over and see what is the matter." With which words he shot off in the direction of some approaching figures and left his providentially supplied substitute to go his way with his companion.

They sought the church-door. Danny was not unduly disturbed. The anchoress not infrequently suffered from illness, but she had, so far never allowed those who ministered to her to break down the dividing wall. She had dragged her bedding under the inner window and been so served in her helplessness. Such was the iron determination of the recluse lady. Danny had heard it all from Sister Perpetua, Dame Catherine's sturdy adherent.

Nicholas wondered what would happen now. He sent up a prayer that he might not have arrived too late with the great amend.

The little sanctuary looked exactly the same. The server knew where to find the vestments and holy vessels—God's Danny was not a little proud of his abilities in serving Mass. On this occasion there was no congregation. The little colony was too much taken up with the arrival of the strayed mariners to remember its religious exercises. So Fra Nicholas stood in the empty church before the familiar altar and said his Mass of thanksgiving, adding a special memento of one suffering sickness of body.

He glanced at the little window-slit in the chancel wall. How near he was to her. It was impossible to realise it. Her physical isolation had always been so complete in its austerity. He breathed forth his Mass, losing himself, as he always did, in the great mystery. Distractions rarely got a hold on the friar who had found his way very near to God—or rather, the distraction ceased to be such, being drawn up, as it were, into the world which he had entered. Thus, even as he lifted the sacred Host at the moment of consecration there floated into his consciousness a sense of proximity to the soul for which he had been making a memento. Many times he had carried the sacred food from the altar to the little window, but now it seemed to him, somewhere dimly in the back of his consciousness, that little window had approached him, or rather, that in looking upon the sacred Host he had localised the anchorhold which in reality enclosed the recluse lady, who for a score of years had dwelt incluse for the love of Christ. Yea, verily, he was looking upon the Anchorhold which containeth all love, and the love of all. Within that circled infinity was neither proximity nor distance, here nor there.

There came a sound through the narrow window as of scraping and dislodging, such as a mason makes when he takes down a wall. They were entering the sanctum sanctorum, the frightened sisters and the young priest. But Fra Nicholas immersed in his Mass, heard nothing. He in sooth had already entered the Anchorhold.

He knelt quietly after Mass making his thanksgiving. Outside there was a hum of voices and the sound of shuffling feet, but Fra Nicholas stayed on, finishing his thanksgiving. The anchoress would be laughing at him for giving thought to so irrelevant a thing as her reputation—what others thought of her. His theology had simplified itself as hers had done. He could express the whole of reality in the words, "Thou and I." He had entered the anchorhold.

Danny, who had slipped out directly after Mass, returned and going up to the priest touched him on the shoulder.

"They have broken the wall and been inside the anchorhold," he said, "and they have found her dead—kneeling up against yon little window with her eyes wide open."

Fra Nicholas rose from his knees and followed the other out. It was no news to him. He would not have it otherwise. There was a small crowd assembled outside the open door of the anchorhold, through which the *débris* of the partitioning wall could be seen. Old sister Perpetua stood there weeping, guarding the sanctities of the death-chamber with fierce fidelity. Felicity, dear soul, who slept near, under one of the mounds, doubtless kept vigil likewise over her pretty one.

Some of the women were on their knees. Others had already possessed themselves of "relics" in the shape of flowers from the anchoress's garden, for a great story had gone abroad to the effect that the benighted fishermen had seen the beacon light burning on St. Catherine's tower at the identical moment, according to the conjectures of those who had examined the body, that the holy woman had passed to her reward. The light had saved the mariners from the quicksands towards which they were drifting, but no man's hand had set fire to the beacon that night, neither had it been seen on land. Moreover the chaplain had happened to pass the night in the little chamber in the tower which he sometimes used as a lodging, and he had heard nothing. He had been belated and it was in passing through the church, late in the night, that he had heard the recluse calling to him from her window. She had told him that she felt herself to be taken for death, and she had prayed to God to send him, and he had come. That was how he came to be there. She had begged to make her confession and to receive her viaticum. So he had shriven her and given her housling. That had been not long before dawn. He had set off at daylight for the convent and told them what had happened, and it had been on his return journey that he had met Fra Nicholas and his companion.

The little cluster of villagers and convent servants was agog with this story. Some would still have it that the mariners were drawing upon their imaginations, and an eager appeal was made to the priest to testify to the truth of their statement.

He stood there in their midst, a commanding figure in his white habit, with the seraphic calm of his countenance in marked contrast to the agitated faces round him. Some of them recognised him as their one-time chaplain, but they found it hard to believe that this man, with his awe-compelling presence, was indeed Nicholas the chaplain of other days.

"Children," Fra Nicholas said, "what thou hast heard is very truth, for I saw the light myself, and most truly it came from the spot where this holy woman was yielding up her soul to God. We were all praying for succour, and succour came. But list ye, and I will tell ye something stranger yet." The listeners pressed nearer. All eyes were fixed on the face of the friar, with its sweet abiding smile.

"A-many years ago," he said, "when I was your chaplain serving yonder altar that same thing happened to me before, for I was young and hot-headed, and filled with the self-spirit of pride and impatience, and my bark was being sucked towards the direful quicksands that the devil doth draw those into who set their ways against those of Holy Church. And lo! in the midst of my dark drifting there sprang up a light from this same holy spot that showed me my error and saved me from the near peril. That light, children," he went on, "was a message of the love of God such as filled my soul with understanding, and it was told to me by her now lying yonder." He glanced wistfully from face to face. "I became a friar in order to preach that same message abroad, and I was sent, bearing that same light—the true faith of Holy Church as she hath ever held it—to other countries in the danger of the quicksands of false teaching. It hath been written in a book which all the world readeth—this revelation made to the holy soul dwelling yonder, forgotten and despised. This strange happening, my children, is one of God's stories, and have I not made it yet more wonderful for ye?"

There was comprehension on a few of the faces, mystification on the others. One thing all grasped alike, the miracle had been duly authenticated by this holy friar who was the most famous preacher of the day. They stood gazing at him with a sort of spiritual embarrassment. The shepherd looked on the little flock, and then he spoke again. "Hers was a great, a mighty soul," he said, "and no doubt a high place is hers in Glory, but she was great in that she had much to combat. 'Twas a generous giver and a valiant fighter that dwelt yonder betwixt four walls—the second man which is of heaven heavenly fighting with the first man Adam. Love, and love only, made her as strong as death. Her place in Heaven shall be high because the conquest was hard. My children, let us kneel down and say a *de profundis* for her most valiant soul."

He knelt down and all present followed suit. The prayer rose as a sobbing murmur. As it ended those who held flowers from the garden path in their hands kissed them. The tears flowed down the furrows in the cheeks of the sea-faring men. It had been a stroke of spiritual genius. Fra Nicholas had preached the anchoress's panegyric, and he had given his hearers a saint whose memory they would cherish with a fierce fidelity as that of a kinswoman—a saint of flesh and blood. He rose to his feet. Was it a coincidence that he had been kneeling on the mound that covered the mortal remains of Felicity, the sharer of the secret of the loose brick?

There was a suddenness and buoyancy in the movement that seemed to lift all the weeping folk kneeling round not only on to their feet but almost up into the air.

He threw his arms out. "And now," he said, "we will sing a *Te Deum* to the great God Who is so wonderful in His saints."

Chapter XXIV

Nunc Dimittis

THE BURYING of the holy anchoress of St. Catherine's was an even greater occasion than the enclosing had been. There had gone abroad the extraordinary story of the beacon light seen at the moment of her death, and the saving of the lives of those at sea, yea that of the famous black friar returning home from the Netherlands, who had testified to the story.

Folks at a distance were beginning to wonder, vaguely, why the holy mother, Dame Catherine, had been allowed to drop out of their ken. The notion had got abroad that she was already dead. Now they were flocking to her burying in crowds, that gave the abandoned highway something of its old appearance—a strange, temporary resurrection from the dead.

The remains of the anchoress were to be laid in the church-yard, not in the undercroft beneath the anchorhold. My lord, the bishop, had so stipulated when he gave his permission for a successor to replace the deceased recluse. Times had progressed since the last enclosing, and the bishop had further stipulated that the new anchoress should have no wall built up to her cell, and furthermore that she should have access to a small garden where she might walk and take the fresh air. His lordship, being a man of advanced ideas, had insisted on all this. Perhaps the new anchoress was a person of less pronounced sanctity than had been the case with the Lady Editha de Beauville; or perhaps she did not possess the latter's faculty for obtaining the thing she desired? At any rate Dame Godiva would inhabit the anchorhold under more modern and commonsense conditions.

The body of the holy mother lay in state in her little cell, surrounded by lights. They had lifted her poor bedding on to a bier and laid thereon the frail attenuated form which they had found kneeling at the little inner window that gave upon Eternity. Her head had fallen forward but the brave blue eyes were wide open. She must have been gazing out on her vista when death came and beckoned her along the pathway. All the village folk, men, women and children, had filed through the opening made by Peter the mason to gaze upon the face of the dead woman and marvel at the sweet, mysterious perfume which filled the place where she lay; and on the occasion of the burial they thronged the churchyard, making a concourse similar to that which had assembled for the enclosing, twenty years before.

This time there was to be a double ceremony for the anchorhold was not to be left empty. The enclosing of Dame Godiva, the holy nun who was to inherit the honour of occupying the cell of Dame Catherine, would take place even as the body of her predecessor was borne forth. There would be a double drama of actual and symbolical death, well suited to the spirit of the dying age—a spirit which would pass with the last of the anchorites, "incluse for the love of Christ."

It was a curious double ceremony. Fra Nicholas, the saint-friar —the most famous preacher in the land at that moment—was to deliver a discourse on the departed. He had ridden back from the North on purpose, accompanied by one Master Roger de Worde, a friend of former days whom he had not met for many years, and Fiddlemee the jongleur, who had pursued him with a message from the dead woman.

The friar was there as the bishop's representative, for all honour was being paid to the inmate of the sequestrated anchorage.

His discourse would be addressed to many persons of high degree as well as to the simple folk. Sir Simon the parson was in attendance with his curates. The nuns' aged chaplain had been brought thither—a silent old man with a sweet child's smile. It would not be in order to vindicate the anchoress, to reinstate her reputation in the eyes of the world, that he would speak—that were an impertinence, and, moreover an impertinence offered to Almighty God as well as the deceased. It would be for the edification of the neighbour that he would tell the story of the anchorhold.

He stood on the path facing the anchorage waiting for the procession approaching from the convent. Dame Godiva, the young contemplative whose life as a choir sister had edified her fellow-religious for many years past, was approaching to assume her new mode of life—the beautiful ideal of spiritual take-and-give which constitutes the life in the anchorhold. The other procession was in waiting at the threshold of the anchorage.

When the first had approached sufficiently near to form part of his audience Fra Nicholas lifted his hand and delivered his discourse. He told his hearers of the woman who had glimpsed the highest and pursued it. How she had made the heroic sacrifice of wealth and position, not content with merely making goodly use of the same, albeit that she had done much good that way. How she had passed by the position even of a noble lady prioress ruling her cloister, and taken herself to yon anchorhold that her giving might be whole and entire—the price of the highest.

And then he told them how God had accepted her good will and had shown her what that All is which must be spent in the purchase of a treasure hidden in a field. He had lured her into the wilderness—aye, and so to do, He had turned the highway from its course. Here the speaker made a wild movement with his arm which swept the gaze of all towards the distant line of white on the green landscape. He had led her on the path of complete renunciation, of denudation, till her very identity was lost. So she had, in sooth, yielded all, sitting there meekly bowing to the circumstances which were God's speech to the soul, until her four happy walls became, as it were, the divine embrace. And at the end her valiant faith had crowned its conquest, for she had deliberately cast away the opportunity for regaining that which she had lost— her good name, her reputation, her identity—yea, that glorious good-will had risen at last against holy Circumstance lest it had robbed her of her treasure—the possession of One whose blissful Name made sweet music in her heart—Jesus!

He ended, and made a sign to the escort of Dame Godiva to approach. The new anchoress held her eyes downcast for she was but leaving one enclosure for another, and it ill-behoved her to forget her holy rule of taking no cognisance of things around her. Many memories would have been revived by a glance at that little grey structure which was to shelter and protect her pearl of great price—sweet and tender memories, not obliterated by the cloud of forgetting which goes with the divine cloud of unknowing, for, like the friar, Godiva had established herself in an anchorhold in which all beauty is enclosed.

But she kept her eyes downcast and saw only the grassy path, until she heard the voice of Fra Nicholas addressing her. This time memory was reawakened by a sense over which she had no means of control, for it had been Nicholas the chaplain who had first brought her hither to see the anchoress when she was a child weeping over a broken pitcher. It was he who had heard her childish confessions and, together with the anchoress, led her to the path which she was pursuing.

The other procession had met them. She saw the feet of those that carried the bier containing the uncovered body of the sleeping anchoress. The latter lay there smiling in her sleep, with her hands crossed over the crucifix on her white-robed bosom. Her thin cheeks retained the soft pink flush, as of sudden pleasure. She might have but dropped asleep a moment since. It was a wondrous sight. But Godiva still held the custody of her eyes until there rang out the voice of Fra Nicholas.

"Lift thine eyes, child, and look upon her whom thou followest that thou mayest learn of peace, and of thine own exceeding reward."

Then, trained to instant obedience, Godiva raised her eyes and looked upon the bier that was being carried to the grave; and as she looked she knew that the vision which she had gazed upon years ago had been no vision, but the face of the holy anchoress herself, looking downward and smiling as she was looking downward and smiling now.

And yet it had been a vision. She had made no mistake, Godiva realised this as she stood taking her fill. This that she was looking upon was no mere earthly beauty but a mystic something—a special gift of the Maker of all beauty. The "magic" which had cast its spell on the pure eyes of the knight, now wending his way on the pilgrim's road—God's glory glinting on a little clay—the dust of one who had cried, "and now I live and yet not I but Christ liveth in me."

The ceremonies were over. The crowd had quietly dispersed. The new anchoress knelt in her cell hugging the fading echoes of the "*In Paradisum deducant te angeli.*" The former anchoress—yea, the former anchoress from her place in Paradise looked downward, smiling at the place of vision. Out in the churchyard the friar lingered. He had caught sight of a familiar figure. Fiddlemee had been conscious of his incongruous garb and had kept in the background. Now he was seated at the far end of the little "weeping acre" with his still-bright eyes fixed on the spot where they had laid the beauteous thing which they had carried forth from the anchorhold. He had his lute on his knee and did not hear the friar approach for he was making music on the strings. Faint music, for Orpheus was suffering from his maltreatment. As the other drew near he caught the words of the song:—"*Nunc dimittis servum tuum Domine.*" Fiddlemee was singing his *Nunc Dimittis*. It was the hour of compline with the King's jongleur.

Fra Nicholas touched him softly on the shoulder. "Brother," he said, "thou hast done well to sing thy *Nunc Dimittis*, for methinks it is time that thou didst seek rest and refreshment. Thou hast laboured well as a good and faithful servant for thy Master, come home with me to the house of my Order and be my clerk and aid me to write the chronicle of yon holy lady. We hold her story between us—thou and I. What I cannot tell thou canst, and what thou wouldst not tell I may, mayhap, supply." He smiled. "Nay," he went on, as the other demurred, "see the rift in the Orpheus hath not healed in spite of the holy mother's glue. His voice is well nigh mute. That meaneth that his master is to lay him aside, or else the glue had surely held good."

A slow smile spread itself over the wrinkled face of the jongleur. "Thou hast put thy case right cunningly, reverend father," quoth he. He struggled to his feet. "I have sung my *Nunc Dimittis* and I will stand by it. And God reward thy charity."

So they left the holy acre in fellowship—the man of God, and the King's jongleur. And of that strange fellowship there came the "Chronicle of Mother Catherine, a devout anchoress dwelling incluse," upon which, if it please his fancy, the reader may consider this story to be founded.

THE END

ALSO BY ENID DINNIS

View a sample chapter from each title at www.staidanpress.com.

THE ROAD TO SOMEWHERE

Richard and Ann discover a real Tudor house in London being sold cheap, complete with leather latch-strings, a tale of hidden treasure, and a wonderful piper. But the treasure turns out to be an old altar-stone. Will it lose them the house and each other, or set them on the real road to Somewhere?

$10.00 — 106 pages. Available at amazon.com.

THE SHEPHERD OF WEEPINGWOLD

Sir Robert Luffkyn, rich grandson of a peasant, has purchased the manor of Weepingwold from the noble but impoverished de Lessels, intending to make the renamed Luffkynwold a busy center of his tanning trade. He sends Petronilla, last de Lessels, to Gracerood, intending her for its future Abbess, and plucks little Brother Kit from the cloister to become the new parson of the long-abandoned church. How will Father Kit fare with the parish and his own soul? What is Petronilla's true vocation? And is there really a witch in the parish?

$14.00 — 202 pages. Available at amazon.com.

OTHER TITLES AVAILABLE FROM ST. AIDAN PRESS

THE QUEEN'S TRAGEDY
by Msgr. Robert Hugh Benson

"Upon the publication of former books of mine several kindly critics remarked that the reign of Mary Tudor told a very different story with regard to the Catholic character. It is that story which I am now attempting to set forth as honestly as I can."

$19.00 — 364 pages. Available at amazon.com.

THE NET
by Agnes Blundell

"Roger felt a freezing dew break out upon his forehead. The net was over him it seemed; in vain he told himself that he could establish his identity. His head was worth forty pounds to the vile creatures at the stair foot, and once in their clutches who knew if he could ever communicate with his friends?... Gaolers and pursuivants alike fattened on the traffic in human life and divided the spoils. Judges were as careless as callous."

$16.00 — 264 pages. Available at staidanpress.com.

THEY MET ROBIN HOOD
by Agnes Blundell

Osmund does a good turn to one of Robin Hood's outlaws and makes friends with the band. But how can outlaws help his family against a friend of Prince John?

$15.00 — 214 pages. Available at amazon.com.

REDROBES
by Fr. Neil Boyton, S.J.

Thirteen-year-old orphan Jacques gets into trouble in Quebec, and decides to run away to Huronia and become an interpreter for his Jesuit guardian, Father John Brebeuf. But his journey along the Iroquois-infested river may not be so easy as he hopes!

$17.00 — 300 pages. Available at amazon.com.

SCOUTING FOR SECRET SERVICE
by Fr. Bernard F. J. Dooley

Frank and George are going to spend their summer vacation in the Adirondacks, thanks to Frank's uncle Ed. But once they get there, they realize something fishy is going on. Can they trust Pete, their Indian guide, or is he mixed up in it too? And is Frank's mysterious uncle really behind it all?

$14.00 — 188 pages. Available at amazon.com.

THE MASTERFUL MONK
by Fr. Owen Francis Dudley

Brother Anselm comes back to England to counter the Atheist's efforts to destroy the influence of Catholic morals. Between his lectures he is drawn into a struggle for the soul of Beauty Dethier, who is Catholic but fascinated by the "freedom" of the world and the Atheist. It will take more than argument to save her from disaster.

$18.00 — 342 pages. Available at amazon.com.

WILL MEN BE LIKE GODS? & THE SHADOW ON THE EARTH
by Fr. Owen Francis Dudley

Father Dudley's first two books on human happiness are published together here—his rare collection of essays together with a novel which illustrates the essays and introduces his most famous character, the Masterful Monk.

$15.00 — 216 pages. Available at amazon.com.

CANDLELIGHT ATTIC & ODD JOB'S
by Cecily Hallack

"I am continually hearing stories—exquisite ones—which would be proof enough to any soul that God is an Infinitely Understanding Person. But usually for the very reason of their nature, they are private—keepsakes between the soul and God."

$14.00 — 192 pages. Available at amazon.com.

THE HAPPINESS OF FATHER HAPPÉ
by Cecily Hallack

Shingle Bay did not know what to make of Fr. Savinius Happé. He was a cheerful, rotund Franciscan, a famous author of books on everything from Etruscan civilization to Alpine meadows to beetles, and someone who had never quite mastered the English language. His jovial demeanor concealed a wisdom that alternately bewildered, astonished, but ultimately won over the people of Shingle Bay.

$10.00 — 112 pages. Available at amazon.com.

THE RED INN OF SAINT LYPHAR
by Anna T. Sadlier

Once Saint Lyphar was a happy village in France, ruled by a generous Marquis and taught by the good Curé. Now the Révolution has put the Curé to death, and the villagers are about to rise under the famous leader Jambe d'Argent. But a Revolutionary spy is lurking near the Inn....

$13.00 — 168 pages. Available at amazon.com.

CON OF MISTY MOUNTAIN
by Mary T. Waggaman

"It had been a long night for Con. Just what had happened to him he was at first too dazed to know. Dennis had flung him into the smoking-room with no very gentle hand, turned the key and left him to himself. And, sinking down dully upon a rug that felt very soft and warm after the hard flight over the mountain, Con was glad to rest his bruised, aching limbs, his dizzy head, without any thought of what was to come upon him next."

$14.00 — 190 pages. Available at amazon.com.

NON-FICTION

THE STORY OF THE WAR IN LA VENDÉE AND THE LITTLE CHOUANNERIE, by George J. Hill, M.A.

The story of the brave French Catholics who rose up in arms against the revolutionary government.

$18.00 — 342 pages. Available at amazon.com.

CATHOLICISM AND SCOTLAND, by Compton Mackenzie

The little known history of the Scots who sought to defend their country and their Faith from the onslaught of Protestantism.

$12.00 — 138 pages. Available at amazon.com.

DOMINICAN SAINTS, by the Novices of the Dominican House of Studies

The astonishing lives of fourteen saints of the Dominican Order, with an encyclical on the Dominican Order by Pope Benedict XV and a list of all the Dominican Saints and Blesseds (as of 1921).

$19.00 — 392 pages. Available at amazon.com.

www.ingramcontent.com/pod-product-compliance
Lightning Source LLC
Chambersburg PA
CBHW051743040426
42447CB00008B/1275

* 9 7 8 0 9 7 1 9 2 3 0 3 4 *